GOD'S GIFT
of
ANGER

GOD'S GIFT
of
ANGER

Doris Moreland Jones

CHALICE PRESS
ST. LOUIS, MISSOURI

© Copyright 2005 by Doris Moreland Jones

All rights reserved. For permission to reuse content, please contact Copyright Clearance Center, 222 Rosewood Drive, Danvers, MA 01923, (978) 750-8400, www.thenewcopyright.com.

Biblical quotations, unless otherwise noted, are from the *New Revised Standard Version Bible*, copyright 1989, Division of Christian Education of the National Council of the Churches of Christ in the United States of America. Used by permission. All rights reserved.

Cover art: PhotoDisc
Cover and interior design: Elizabeth Wright

This book is printed on acid-free, recycled paper.

Visit Chalice Press on the World Wide Web at
www.chalicepress.com

10 9 8 7 6 5 4 3 2 1   05 06 07 08 09

Library of Congress Cataloging-in-Publication Data

Jones, Doris Moreland.
  God's gift of anger / Doris Moreland Jones.
    p. cm.
  ISBN 13: 978-0-827212-49-6 (pbk. : alk. paper)
  ISBN 10: 0-827212-49-6
  1. Anger—Religious aspects—Christianity. I. Title.
BV4627.A5J657 2004
248.4—dc22
                                              2004014435

Printed in the United States of America

Contents

1 The Gift of Anger   1

2 The Denial of Anger   11

3 The Escalations of Anger Denied   19

4 Other Negative Choices Concerning Anger   31

5 Making Positive Choices about Our Anger   49

6 Answers to Frequently Asked Questions about Anger   67

7 Children and Anger   87

8 Practical Advice for Claiming the Gift of Anger   103

1

The Gift of Anger

Of all the emotions we feel, from excitement to hopelessness, none causes us as much difficulty as anger. Anger can clear the air, give us courage to admit what we honestly feel. It can break through a problem, and it can stir us to a long overdue action. Or it can eat away inside us, destroy relationships, or even maim ourselves and others. Anger, when expressed appropriately, is healthy. Anger, when denied, repressed, or unleashed aggressively, can become a very destructive force.

For many of us it is not anger that is the problem, but how we express it, and how we react to its pervasive presence in our lives. This book is about God's *gift* of anger and the many ways we relate to it, both negative and positive, in our lives. It is a journey of discovery that I invite you to take with me as we move from denial to affirmation and finally to practical tools for harnessing this strange gift.

Some of us grew up with unhealthy ideas about anger. For many of us anger was a bad word in our family of origin. Growing up in a southern culture, I learned early that anger was not feminine, so even when I was angry I could not admit that I was. Showing anger was akin to being rude. Some families even let it be known that anger was a sign of mental instability. It is not surprising that anger is such a problem in interpersonal relationships. Others had another set of rules to live by. Those rules emphasized that it was not only all right to show anger, but the more the better. If anyone expressed anger, you were to retaliate with more anger.

Anger is often used as a mask when one feels embarrassed, ashamed, or fearful. Men, often feel anger is a more acceptable emotion than what they perceive as the softer emotions, such as tenderness, love, or caring. It is as if real men do not show tender emotions. Somehow, to do so might show them as "wimps." It is unfortunate that females learn to mask anger by using other emotions such as concern or disappointment. Hence the familiar statement, "I am not mad; I am hurt." Anger is often directed against those who have less power than we do. Hence, bosses are not challenged, but the grocery checker or the gas station attendant or the paper carrier receive anger that is not really meant for them. Those who feel powerless in the chain of command also sometimes, unfortunately, take their anger out on spouses, children, or pets.

When we are still learning to recognize and honor anger's voice, we hesitate. Do I read anger into everything? Jan L. Richardson, in her book *Sacred Journeys: A Woman's Book of Daily Prayer,* writes about Mary and Martha's anger when Lazarus died, then wonders if it is about their anger or her own anger, or that of many women she has known. She writes, that the taboos against our feeling and expressing anger are so powerful that even *knowing* when we are angry is not a simple matter.[1] Because the very possibility that we are angry often meets with rejection and disapproval from others, it is no wonder that it is hard for us to know, let alone admit, that we are angry.

Anger is not a sinful emotion. But how we act when we are angry may well be a sin. The Greek language, which has three words for love, has only two words for anger: *thumos,* an anger that blazes up and then quickly dies down, and *orge,* an anger that stays, rages, and harbors ill will. *Orge* is the most difficult for a person to work through, and is more of a problem for family, coworkers, or neighbors. The ill will and feelings of revenge can be almost a comfort to the person feeling full of rage or hostility. *Thumos* blazes up so quickly—and then just as

---

[1] Jan L. Richardson, *Sacred Journeys: A Woman's Book of Daily Prayer* (Nashville: Upper Room Books, 1994), 154.

rapidly dies down—that the one feeling this anger often assumes she has no problem with anger. Family members or the people she works with would be quick to respond with disagreement, since they never know when such a person will blow. Both kinds of anger need to be examined and decisions must be made about better patterns for dealing with them.

We may recognize our anger, but be overwhelmed with the enormity of it. It overpowers and frightens us. In working with groups where I we try to help members identify their feelings, after they have told me of an event I often ask them what they are feeling. A frequent answer is, "I don't know. I really do not know what I am feeling." I try to help them to be more specific by asking if they are mad, sad, glad, or surprised. The enormity of their anger makes it easier to confess to being sad, rather than claim their anger. Or they may admit to frustration, but declare they are not mad. Despite anger being a common, normal emotion, we must admit it gets very bad press. Whether we feel mild annoyance or a raging fury, if we have been taught anger is bad, or a sign of weakness, or something to be hidden, we continue to try to hide our emotions. Attempts to stamp out our emotions inevitably lead to failure.

Anger frequently is disguised as something more acceptable, such as shock, fear, grief, despair, hopelessness, self-hate, hyperactivity, and busyness. We must learn to listen to our anger to hear the soft notes, the plaintive notes, those that sob, notes that thunder, and notes that fairly crackle. All anger is not black or bright red. Some of it shimmers like tears, while some is a dull brown shade of hopelessness.

There are clues that our bodies, the viscera, give us when we feel angry. If we take them one by one, they give us a message. The tight band around my head after I have been in the company of a person whom I perceive has put me down. The headache that keeps me awake after the meeting where I fear I was not heard but patted on the head. My stomach, which is cramping and sour after hearing an explanation that does not tell me why our church does not have enough money to help the inner-city kids, but does have enough to re-carpet the offices. You have your own clues—the backaches, the runny nose, sleeplessness, the tension headache, or a one-day virus where your get-up-and-go has gone. Or it may be constipation, diarrhea, a gallbladder attack, or a summer cold, but we must learn to read the signs, and know if they are visceral clues to our anger.

Body language may give away our anger, no matter how much we deny it. The fast trip to the restroom with a rigid back after a confrontation with the boss telegraphs anger. When a coworker or friend asks, the person responds, "The boss does not understand me." That may well be true, but it is not germane. Denying anger does not take away our angry feelings.

Some say that anger has an olfactory dimension also. Waves of smell emit from the one consumed with rage until the very air is charged, while righteous indignation comes out in a soft whoosh of frail smells that conceals the ardor aroused. The taste of anger may be metallic, filled with bile, strongly acidic, or the stale taste of nausea; but whatever the taste, it is unforgettable and lasting. When we have spent time learning to know ourselves, the clues to our own anger are God-given and unmistakable.

Anger can be a great source of empowerment, or denying it can be a way of accepting powerlessness, which gives the trump card for anger to destroy us. We have the power to transform our differences, but this is not automatic. Our own creativity helps us to alter and change our insight into power.

Anger is not the opposite of love, for the opposite of love is indifference. To be angry is to care tremendously. It is a signal that your caring extends beyond polite conversation, and that you are willing to risk a confrontation to share how you feel and how you see the issues involved. Anger is active—that is, if it is to accomplish anything. Anger signals loud and clear that all is not well in our relations to others or the world around us. Anger connects us to others, even when we do not agree. There is energy in anger that lifts us to engage with others and to seek dialogue, and sometimes even a solution.

Security vs. Insecurity

Every emotion, even anger, has a result directly related to the well-being of humanity. For instance, loneliness brings persons together as they seek the company of others, and can lead to marriage and procreation. Guilt helps us to keep order and to restrain our behavior. It is why we stop at red lights, even when we are in a hurry. It gives us a sense of order, which we need to survive. Fear signals danger and is the body's warning. When our children were very young, we were concerned when they seem to have no sense of fear as they floated into the deep water or chased a ball into the street. Anger is no exception. It has many functions. Often it gives us the push needed to fight injustice, prejudice, and even struggle against the elements. Adrenaline rushes through our bodily systems, enabling us to accomplish the impossible. We hear of persons swimming farther than they ever had before as they bring a drowning person to shore. Weak people without stamina, who normally could not move half that weight, lift cars from trapped persons. In anger arousal the body produces adrenaline that has a numbing effect on the body which allows us to keep on even when it causes us pain.

Chemicals have a way of magnifying behavior and emotions. Alcohol and drugs can cause persons to cry copiously, and at times inappropriately, or they may laugh in loud and raucous ways out of proportion to an event. Anger may become irrational, ending in blind rage. The relationship between anger and drugs or alcohol is very complex. For those whose family of origin taught that anger was off-limits, using alcohol or drugs offers a way to express anger without being responsible for it. After an event they easily say, "Gee, that wasn't me, it was just the booze or the pills talking." Some folks take a tranquilizer if they feel they are going to "lose their temper." Others may use alcohol to bury emotions. Of course, that does nothing to resolve the reason for the anger, and only stockpiles anger that comes out later, often at a most inappropriate time.

I remember a client from years back who would never claim his anger, but always acted it out. He had drunk his anger for more than thirty-five years. With sobriety he had failed to learn new ways to deal with his anger, which had turned into rage. When he and his wife began to have serious marriage problems, he was so incensed he went to a bar and drank himself into oblivion. He was chagrined and embarrassed the next day when he called his sponsor, who referred him to me. We spent many hours in therapy while he learned healthy and productive actions to dispel his anger. His wife came in also and learned how she enabled his putting his anger inside, as well as how to recognize her own anger.

As each learned to deal with his or her own anger, they each learned about individual insecurity. Feeling insecure magnified feelings of inferiority. Trying always to be in control, to have the perfect answer, and to never let the others know about their uncertainty led to further insecurity. The reverse was also true. As unresolved anger was no longer a pervasive part of their life, they learned to feel secure being who they were, or as Frederick Buechner phrases it, "being comfortable in their own skin." My client decided to coach a church softball team where he dealt with irate parents who thought their child was a Babe Ruth in the making. As the client and I talked about it he said the coaching was going well. He knew the parents were insecure about their parenting, and he remembered personally what that was like. He grinned, saying he might refer some of them for counseling.

Unresolved anger is a relapse trigger that can lead to guilt, resentment, and shame. It can lead to an increased use of drugs or alcohol to avoid the so-called bad feelings. It may also be a rationalization for the use of chemicals: "I deserve a drink. Look at the way they treat me. I'll only have one." If you are looking for an excuse for substance abuse, it can always be found, just as you can always find someone to blame for your actions. Insecure persons usually do not accept responsibility for their actions. In fact, over time they come to believe life is out to get them, and they are not to blame. Secure persons look at the happening, weigh the pros and cons, and then decide on the best course of action. This may well mean they have to accept blame for what has gone wrong, and admit they made a mistake. If someone else has erred, they confront the person unemotionally and look for a solution. Those who are secure do not have to be right all the time. Belligerence or lassitude rarely is a good beginning to resolve problems

Secure people quickly find out that there is a difference between taking care of oneself and dumping on others. Having the last word is overrated and overdone. Dealing with our anger is vital, but we must learn to do so without dumping on others.

To let our anger out is important, but we do not have to be destructive as we do so. Anger and violence are not the same thing. Anger is wrongly used as a justification for violence. Often we hear, "I just lost control," or "I was in a blind rage," or "I saw red and I don't remember anything after that." We can never deal constructively with anger until we accept the idea that violence is wrong. No one, absolutely no person, deserves to be a victim of violence. Refraining from violence is absolutely necessary.

Disagreement in our churches and denominations can bring on bitter disputes. Even on church-related electronic bulletin boards or chat rooms, people call others vicious names and discount their parentage, all because the other does not see "right" as what they know "right" to be. Where in scripture does it say that we are always right, and if anyone disagrees with us, they are wrong? We suffer from insecurity if "everyone" must agree with our stand on everything.

God must like diversity! When we look about us we see a world of differing colors in nature (often ten to twelve shades of green alone) and a variety of people—fat and thin, light and dark, smiling and frowning, short and tall, bright and struggling, friendly and grumpy. God gave us free will in an amazing act of trust. We make a decision and then we are responsible for that decision, whether it is good or not so good. God loves us enough to trust us, yet we do not trust others unless they are in agreement with us. Can we not be secure in God's demonstrated love for us, without condemning those who disagree with us?

What Are My Priorities?

Is my top priority being liked by everyone? Is this the principle that governs my life? Do I fear my own anger because it might bring disapproval? Could it be that if I acknowledge my anger, I will see the necessity for change in my life? It is easy to invalidate our own experience of anger: Is my anger legitimate? Do I have a right to be angry? What good will it do if I get angry? What's the use of my getting angry anyway? These questions can be an excellent way of silencing ourselves and shutting off our anger.

In Harriet Lerner's book *The Dance of Anger* she reminds us to question the questions. She makes the point that anger is neither legitimate nor illegitimate, nor is it, in and of itself, either meaningful or pointless. As we say so frequently, anger just is. Intrinsically it is neither right nor wrong. Lerner says: "Anger is something we feel. It exists for a reason and always deserves our respect and attention. We all have a right to *everything* we feel—and certainly our anger is no exception."[2]

Other questions about our anger are appropriate to ask. Sometimes our anger is free-floating anger. That is, we are out of sorts and are looking for a place to put our anger and we are not too particular about where it lands. This may be conscious or unconscious.

Boundaries

We must learn to put boundaries on our anger—not the kind of boundaries that say certain subjects or emotions are off limits, but rather boundaries against "shoddy shots" or dirty tricks. In counseling I frequently experience an event in which one spouse sets the other up for a cheap shot. When I identify the behavior, they often feign surprise. Hitting below the belt needs be outside the boundary of acceptable behavior. The guidelines must include a moratorium on old arguments that have never been resolved. Something that happened during the honeymoon is not a valid topic to discuss twenty years later If discussions are to be fruitful, agreement needs to be reached that *feelings* are to be talked about, not the *failings* of the other person. Honesty is mandatory if communication is to happen.

Couples, families, or roommates often set their own rules for fairness: no arguing in front of outsiders, no walking out in the middle of a discussion, and no new rules as the discussion continues. Remember, we argue or fight or discuss for good reasons, not bad ones. We need to know why we are expressing our anger, and what we hope to gain by doing so. Making a list, thinking about our anger in a quiet time, and looking to see if our emotion is out of proportion to the event are all good patterns to follow so that our anger is productive. Confronting situations when they occur, rather than letting them build, can keep

---

[2]Harriet Lerner, *The Dance of Anger: A Woman's Guide to Changing the Patterns of Intimate Relationships* (New York: HarperCollins, 1997), 4.

resentment down, but we must be careful to *only* deal with this one situation.

Responsibility

We have to take responsibility for our anger. Whether it is justified or not, our anger comes from inside us, not from other people. Their behavior may spark our anger, but it is our anger, and we choose how we deal with it. It is unfair to place our anger on another, for this really is a way of refusing to deal with our own anger. The "blaming game" is unfair, such as, "This time you have pushed me too far!" or "If you don't stop provoking me, I can't be responsible for what happens." Such ultimatums are an exercise in trying to blame someone else for what we are feeling.

Taking responsibility for our anger is mature and honest. An "I" statement about our feelings, which after all is our area of expertise, can expedite a disagreement. To say, "You make me so mad" sets up an argument. Instead, we can be open and say, "When you talk about me as if I am not present, I feel deep resentment." If you know yourself well, you may mention that such behavior was common in your family of origin, and it brings up harsh memories. When we tell another person how to behave, we're setting ourselves up as an expert on their behavior. Stating how their behavior incites our feelings is a simple account of facts. Then the decision is how best to deal with what we have learned.

With these initial considerations in mind, let us embark upon our journey together.

2

The Denial of Anger

Strongly entrenched angry behaviors do not fit our image of self, so we are tempted to deny them completely or rationalize them away. We can become obsessive in denying what we believe to be less than pristine emotions. Some emotions are encouraged as we grow and develop, but anger usually is not. Our children may receive dual messages when we strongly discourage their temper tantrums, then exhibit our own anger in loud and rude ways.

The temptation of our culture, and one that is sometimes encouraged by the church, is to deny any feelings we believe to be negative. Of course, if we deny our negative feelings we are never called on to work through them. We can be pious and call our anger "hurt," gain sympathy, and never have to own our broken humanity. That may help us to "feel better" about ourselves, or feel we are better than others. But does it help us on the way to being all that God created us to be?

Twice in my ministry I have directed counseling centers that were a part of major not-for-profit hospitals. This placed me in middle management at meetings in which I frequently experienced administrators denying their anger. At one early morning meeting, the president was especially caustic to a department head. As we left the meeting room and wended our way through the maze of hospital corridors, the department head under siege said, "I asked him to help me understand why he was so angry. But he denied his anger." One of my colleagues muttered, "Well, he had better tell his face, because everything in his body language declared anger, as well as the pulse jumping in his neck, and his refusal to look you in the eye communicated something was amiss." Denying our anger leaves clues: voice pitched higher, red face, agitation, glowering, body posture, and clenched teeth or arms wrapped around one's body. It may be time for all of us to "tell our face," or to begin working through our denial.

Do you ever overhear little vignettes while you are sitting at a table alone, waiting for a friend or spouse to join you for lunch? Having been in a position where I traveled and often ate dinner or breakfast alone, I became fascinated with how much I overheard as I awaited my meal. If I had a newspaper or book, I was invisible. I heard an amazing number of stories and quarrels, and experienced a rich course in interpersonal relationships.

A man alone, waiting, watching the entryway, drumming on the table cloth, told the server that his wife was always late, only to feign a lack of interest when she arrived. She tried to apologize, but he brushed her off. He was silent, ignoring her attempts at conversation. As the meal progressed he refused dessert, despite her assertion that he loved dessert. He either ignored her or by turns was rude. They walked out as I did. He brought up her habitual lateness, but he denied having any anger with his wife. As they both sullenly walked away, it seemed a shame they could not have talked about what happened, and then enjoyed each other and their dinner.

In a hotel coffee shop two men were arguing about the best way to get to an industrial park that was their sales destination. Each was certain his way was the best way. Their argument was repeated over and over. Finally they asked their server the best way to get to the industrial park. The server took a napkin and drew a simple map showing where they needed to go. Then to my surprise, they continued to argue, each pointing to the napkin and saying that was the way he had suggested all the time. As they left, they had their arms around each other's shoulders saying, "Sure is good that we never get mad over our differences."

Denial is clearly seeing the faults and foibles of others but never taking a look at our own. Others get angry, but not us. Anger is one of the most often denied emotions. It is all right to be frustrated, miffed, put out, put upon, but never angry. Hostility, rage, and anger are the emotions that we hide from others and often from ourselves. We erroneously perceive that if we do not admit it, it is not so.

This and other perceptions are colored by what have learned from childhood on into adolescence.

Denial's Roots

None of us had perfect parents, nor did we have perfect childhoods. And as difficult as it is to admit, none of us is a perfect parent. We give our children structure and values, but not without also giving them some quirks and issues they may struggle to deal with for a long time.

Certain admonitions we received in childhood may not be true or even make sense to our adult minds. Yet somewhere inside, we may still accept them as absolute certainties or facts. They rest in our unconscious and play a part in our reacting to certain stimuli.

We must examine the myths that may unconsciously guide our actions even as adults. We can hold our myths up to the light of truth and perhaps expose them as myths that could still be guiding our actions even today. Otherwise, they may become a burden we cannot lay down.

If as a child you were told you must never be angry, it may have become a guiding force in how you choose to live life. It is time, past time, to look at the covert teachings, as well as our assumptions, to see if we give them too much credibility. Is it not time for "the truth (that) will make you free?" (Jn. 8:32).

I have a friend who has accepted an old myth from her family that *nice people do not get angry,* a myth that causes her to have sleepless nights. Being perceived as nice was a cardinal rule in her family of origin.

I met her for lunch recently. She is invariably prompt, with little tolerance for those who are not. This time my friend was fifteen minutes late, and I inquired if there was a problem. She looked frazzled and mumbled her apologies. She played with her food and had difficulty sustaining a conversation. I urged her to share what was wrong. She told me she had used valet parking at a medical center and the valet service had misplaced her car. I responded, "How could they lose your car? Are you angry?" She carefully explained she was not angry, and questioned why I should think she was. Then she spent some minutes telling me how she had conquered anger. Since I was not her therapist, I did not pursue the issue. I could have made her aware that she was unable to eat her lunch or be present during a conversation, or that she appeared overly defensive. But her myth from childhood was in control: "Nice people do not get angry."

Displacement

Displacement is one of ways in which we attempt to deny the anger we're feeling. Several years ago, a man was giving a presentation to a group of chaplains. He projected the image of someone rather full of himself, to put it mildly. He pontificated at length, then asked for questions. Each questioner was cut off or put down. One of the chaplains asked if he were angry. The speaker denied anger, and asked why the question was asked of him. The more the chaplain responded, the angrier the speaker became. The trained chaplain said bluntly, "Well, it seems to me you came here with a mad in your pocket." The speaker flushed, taking quick, shallow breaths. The moderator tactfully said the time was up.

At lunch I sat with the chaplain who had asked the speaker about his anger. I asked about the phrase he had used, "having a mad in your pocket." He said where he was from in western Kentucky it was a common phrase, meaning someone who was displacing anger rather than working it through. I was fascinated by this colloquial expression that expresses so well the displacement of anger.

Sometimes sarcasm becomes the tool for displacing anger, and may take on a very caustic tone. Teasing can be vicious and demeaning, with the one doing the teasing casting aspersions on the sense of humor of the person being teased. Remarks such as: "Ah, come on, can't you take a joke? I was just teasing. Don't be such a wimp. I didn't mean any harm. Why can't you grow up and be like everyone else? You have to learn to accept teasing." Such remarks are usually made from a "one-up" position, with the person with the power putting down the powerless individual. Laughing at someone is not really funny. It is a cruel and cowardly way of expressing our anger. It behooves all of us to check out how we use sarcasm and humor, lest we become unknowingly cruel.

Silence is one of the cruel forms of the displacement of anger. It is so easy to be silent in a disagreement, and even feel holy and righteous about not responding, but if used repeatedly it can become a ploy to win without firing a shot. The silent person never has to apologize. He never says anything in anger, for he never says anything. The verbal partner in the dialogue often overstates her opinions, trying to get some response from her silent cohort. Silence is not golden in communication. It is deadly. The exception to this is when you are trying to dialogue with someone who is a substance abuser, a tired and sleepy child, or someone who is ill, or when you are both overwrought. Using silence to feel superior is not fighting fair. Check your use of silence to see if you are taking unfair advantage of your verbal opponent, while smugly feeling self-righteous. When the silent one repeatedly pushes the verbal partner to over-emote, sometimes the wrong one says, "I'm sorry." If you are silent because you are afraid to speak up, then seek help from your pastor or a good friend as soon as possible.

The hail-fellow-well-met attitude can be another displacement of anger. The chipper, ever-happy person may well be hiding behind a facade, fearing what would happen if he ever let out his real feelings. So-called negative emotions may not have been allowed in his family of origin, so he became used to stifling any emotion he could not smile about. Life being what it is, there are many less than perfect events. If we learn early on that we do not always get what we want, we are better equipped to deal with what life brings us. One of the much-used clichés says, "all sunshine makes a desert," and cliché or not, it is true. We can be happy and joyful knowing tomorrow may be very different, and being open to each new event. Some of us were taught that it is more Christian to smile than to frown, but if we are to be all that God created us to be, we must be open to having and using a whole range of emotions, and this includes anger.

Displacement of anger may be through the act of spending money: a bigger house, a faster automobile, a grander vacation.

One client told me, "I may be divorced, but my daughter will have every advantage, and if that means borrowing money to take her to California, then I'll just have to borrow money." I asked her if her former husband could help financially with the trip if she were determined to go. Then she said, "You just don't get it, do you? The idea is show him up! I want to do what he can't do." She was locked in her anger, which she denied. While legally divorced, she was still tied her former husband by her anger; therefore, emotionally she was not divorced. Until she can work through her anger with him, forgive him, and more importantly, forgive herself, she is caught in a tug-of-war where she complains, "Why can't things ever work out right for me? It's just not fair." And she refuses to look deep inside herself, where she might find the answers.

Perfection and Anger

Denied anger allows us to feign perfection and keep the fantasy intact. The need to be perfect is demanding and at times all-consuming. How hard it is to admit we are wrong. I have clients who say the words just stick in their throats. It is as if admitting wrongdoing would diminish one's very self. If in our family of origin it was an ordinary practice for someone to say: "I'm sorry. I was wrong. Can you forgive me?" then it is probably easier for you to apologize. But if your spouse, boss, or tennis partner was reared in an atmosphere where one never admitted wrongdoing so that nobody could get the upper hand, then for them to admit wrongdoing is as painful as having an abscessed tooth pulled.

A couple who came to me for marriage counseling several years ago were delightful people, and well liked by others. But they were regular bridge players, and there the trouble began. Not only were they regular bridge players, they each believed they played championship bridge. Session after session they had a postmortem about their bridge game of the past week. Neither was ever wrong. The other was never right. We seemed to be at a stalemate. I suggested they never again partner with each other. For them it was a radical idea, but they agreed to try. After a few weeks they began to complain about their current bridge partners. When I asked them to explain, they went on at great length about the mistakes, stupid errors, and gross incompetence of their partners. This dialogue frequently alluded to the competence of their former partnership with each other. Fortunately, I had taped this session. When their time was up I took the tape out of the machine, and assigned homework of listening to the tape before their next session with me. At their next appointment they came in holding hands. They had finally heard not just the negatives, but the positives from each other. With that they slowly learned to admit their faults and mistakes in bridge, and more importantly in life.

Perfectionism is caught more than taught. If as a child, your best was never good enough, then you were indoctrinated early into perfectionism. If you got an A- on a test, you were not praised, but instead asked why you didn't get an A. If you played in a recital and messed up one part, that was all that was talked about after the recital. "Good enough" is fine for other folk, but never for a perfectionist. Being right is vital to them. When you try to point out an error, he is incensed, insisting he is right. My secretary told me of an incident where a client insisted he had an appointment with me. The secretary explained that his appointment was actually the following day. He roared, "My appointment is today. I'll prove it to you." He whipped out his appointment card, and his face fell. He said, "How can this be? This card says my appointment is tomorrow at this time. I just don't understand how this can be." When the client left, he was totally bewildered, she reported. His background left no room for errors.

One of my young friends says in his family, perfection was the minimum standard. In Matthew 5:48 it says, "Be perfect, therefore, as your heavenly Father is perfect." But is Jesus' definition of perfection the same as ours? My Greek is a little rusty, but as I read it, Christ was talking of being complete, mature, grown up. We use it to mean being perfect or without flaw, even though we know there are no flawless people. Why do imperfect parents feel they must mold perfect children? Cameron Manifold, in an unpublished manuscript titled, "The Trouble with Being Perfect," says: "The difficulty with our desire to be perfect is that it is both impossible and unnecessary. We are made perfect through grace rather than by our own efforts. This is what makes being perfect impossible. God loves us from the beginning so our desire to be perfect in order that God will love us makes the whole affair unnecessary. God loves us already. If someone requires that we be perfect before we can be loved, we can know that we will never be loved by that one." Indeed, this is what makes being perfect impossible. And unnecessary.

It is a paradox that the other side of perfectionism is procrastination. Of course, this is often the result of others holding high expectations of us. We realize we can never meet their expectations, so we procrastinate until the last minute, burning the midnight oil to prove how hard we are working. Then we say we could have done a really outstanding job if we had had more time. We tell ourselves that it is all right if it is not superior, since we know we have it in us to do better. One of the problems with perfectionism is we get used to waiting until the last minute, and still doing a creditable job. Thus we may count on being late in order to achieve the adrenaline high that comes when we are working against a deadline. We may say we are angry because other people expect so much of us, but it is our drive to achieve perfection. Our anger usually is focused "out there" but it belongs to us. It behooves us to own it, ask for forgiveness, admit our weakness, and know we do not have to be perfect to be perfectly loved by God.

3

The Escalations of Anger Denied

Entrenched anger behaviors do not fit our image of ourselves. We deny that we carry such strong feelings—feelings we may perceive as being negative. We are quick to try to rationalize away any suggestion that we are carrying around repressed rage, hostility, anger—and most assuredly we are not filled with fury or wrath. In this process we further suppress our feelings, but these strong emotions are not readily ignored or cast out. Developing new attitudes and behavior requires hard work and continuous effort.

A new client told me in an intake interview that she never gets angry, but does get *wrathy* sometimes. I asked her to repeat what she said, and she did. Then I asked her what this word *wrathy* meant. (By the way, to my surprise, *wrathy* is in the dictionary. I was astonished to hear her say it was just her way of talking about herself when she was upset. I asked her to look up *wrath, wrathful,* and *wrathy* in her dictionary. She was appalled to read that being *wrathy* was a desire to punish, get even, and look for a way to extract revenge. In addition, it implied extreme anger. She said in her family of origin, anger was never tolerated or approved, but one could be *wrathy.* Without a doubt, this was a false way to deny strong feelings or emotions. The anger that was a no-no in her family was mild compared to wrath or being wrathful. We often go to great lengths to find a displacement for our anger.

Mostly because of their upbringing, some persons simply will not admit feelings of anger. Anger, or any of its derivations, becomes a very powerful control issue with parents or authority figures. Thus, even to talk about anger you need a new language. I normally ask new clients, in their initial interview, how they deal with their anger. Many clients strongly deny they have any anger in their life. Some clients tell me they are frustrated or stressed out, but never angry. They may admit to getting upset, but they strongly deny that they ever feel anger. To them anger is a grievous wrong, and one they will never admit is a part of their life. Often they quote and misquote scripture to back up their position.

The denial of anger starts early, as the plethora of anger-based emotions (shown in such behaviors as temper tantrums) are discouraged by parents. Children can receive are rebuked for showing any kind of anger, then hear parents yell, "We'll have no more scenes like this. Go to your room and don't come out until you can act *right*." Or if a child makes an angry face, she may hear, "What if your face froze like that? You don't ever want anyone to see you looking that way." How rare it is for a parent or a teacher to validate a child's expression of anger. If, as parents or grandparents, we can be healthy enough to respond, "I know you are mad, and it is all right to be mad, but it is not acceptable to hit someone. Please go to your room now, and in a few minutes we will talk about some better choices to express how you feel." To have our feelings acknowledged encourages our self-worth. It allows the feelings, but discourages the tantrums.

My husband and I were breakfasting in a hotel coffee shop in a large city. The booths were very close together, and the conversation between two adults, with a small boy trying to get their attention, was easy to overhear. The server approached the table and asked the boy what he wanted. The woman said, "He wants—" But the server again asked the boy what he wanted. He was so overcome with surprise that someone was listening to him that he must have said the first thing he could think of, "I'll have a hamburger." The server immediately called it back to the cook. The small boy beamed, "She thinks I am real!" How much our children need to feel they are real. How much we need to own our feelings, and help our children own their feelings—positive as well as negative.

Children may develop a pseudo-self to mask those parts of self they have learned by experience are not acceptable. It minimizes punishment, but part of the inner self is lost as they seek to fit the parental mold. This can produce hostile adults. Who among us has not served on boards, committees, or in small groups with someone whose free-floating anger fastened on each issue that was discussed or proposed? If we find ourselves being the one who opposes every action or each proposal, it is time we examine what is going on in our internal space. It is decision time. Do we resign from the group, or do we take a hard look at how often we are angry?

It is vital to remember that feelings are just that—feelings. Rather than being ashamed of our feelings, we need to examine them. It is normal to feel angry at times, just not all the time. It is also normal to feel joy and happiness, but no one can expect to feel euphoric at all times. Life is filled with loss from death, divorce, or disaster. Life is not always fair. No one can escape downward emotions. If we cannot ever feel sadness, we are bordering on being out of touch with reality.

Almost all of us have fears, hurts, and anger from childhood that do not magically evaporate as we grow older. Oddly enough, when we reach a certain level of insight, or circumstances cause us enough pain, we reach a level of maturity and awareness that allows us to look deeply within. When this time comes we have an opportunity to heal the pain and cast out the fears we have held so long.

What does anger mean to you? What images come to your mind when anger is mentioned? Is it chaos? Or darkness? Hate, rage, or fury? Does it bring to mind violence, belligerence, irate persons? Do you believe that anger is to be avoided at all costs? Do you say that anger brings more heat than light, and who needs more darkness in a world that already contains too much darkness?

Anger is one of the most prevalent human emotions. But as we have seen, it is also one of the most denied emotions. Anger seems to have a different connotation for each of us. Some view anger as an irrational emotion that supplants reason, accompanied by physiological and biological changes. Others try to act as if anger does not exist in their world. And anger denied surely deepens into other emotions even more potentially destructive.

Rage

Rather than dealing with our feelings, which often are legitimate, we often ignore them or stuff them inside, adding to our deposit of previously suppressed feelings. Rage usually comes out of feelings that we believe have not been dealt with fairly, a perception that may or may not be legitimate. Rage sometimes is compared with madness. The word *rabid* is used to indicate uncontrolled raging fury.

So-called *nice people* who claim they are never angry always blame their feelings of anger or rage on the actions of others. They are always *acted upon;* never are they the acting party. There are many connotations to anger; thus, when many persons think of anger, they are really recalling rage. Since rage brings behavior they want to avoid, their automatic desire is to suppress their feelings. They lose the opportunity to experience the gift of anger. Instead of suppressing the anger, new ways of responding to the emotion should be explored, developed, and practiced. It is worth the effort involved.

Some persons use alcohol to vent or even heighten their rage. They protect themselves from dealing with any repercussions, declaring they did not mean to hurt your feelings; it was only the *booze* talking. Often they deny meaning any of the things they said while drinking. It is a *safe* way of not having to be responsible for their actions. Such behavior can become habitual, causing great problems in a marriage or other interpersonal relationships.

Another protection used by those who never want to claim their own rage is to tell someone off, then fall back on ethnicity or family heritage as a defense. Excuses fall easily from their lips as they claim that this is just the way it is if you are Italian, or Irish, or—you fill in the blank. They add, "That's the way it is in our family. We all shout at each other, and it doesn't mean anything." In reality, it is another way of making hurtful remarks without being accountable.

Anger in any form was not acceptable in my family of origin. I heard injunctions such as "Nice persons don't get angry" and "Christians don't get angry." "Young ladies do not show anger if they want to be invited again." Since it was not acceptable to show anger, I stuffed it inside myself. I felt anger, of course, but I learned not to express it in any way. I had learned well. My internalized anger grew, gathered some resentment along the way, was flavored with a touch of bitterness, and had new angers stuffed in from time to time. Eventually some small, seemingly unimportant event would trigger my repressed anger. Then my anger would come rumbling and tumbling out like the eruption of Mount St. Helens. And I would make an ash of myself. The strong internalized emotions gathered force and came out with vehemence.

The frenzy passed, and acting within family norms, I quickly apologized. Then I immediately began to stockpile my anger for the next explosion, feeling chagrin and embarrassment that I had not lived in a Christian manner. Small wonder anger is often described as feeling as if your emotions are squeezing your chest. I was an adult in graduate school before I learned anger was a good gift. What a revelation! A gift of freedom. I could allow myself to feel without blowing up to relieve the pressure.

Later I learned what happened when I repressed what I thought was anger. My anger was not exactly anger. The uncontrolled raging feelings came from not acknowledging my displeasure at opposition or trouble. It was fighting back at what seemed unjust or mean. Rage is what happens to ordinary anger that is not dealt with. It may come from a feeling of being powerless. If my myths or early childhood injunctions are in charge, then I am not in charge, but am powerless, bound by the injunctions. Logic pays no part in this feeling of powerlessness.

Hostility

When rage is repressed and not dealt with it becomes hostility. Hostility is an accumulative phenomenon. New events and issues come to lodge in this accumulative mass and the storehouse is enlarged. This takes place usually at an unconscious level. Hostility is all the feelings of anger and rage in a pressure cooker. In the right environment or when an opportunity occurs, the seething hostility erupts with explosive force. The hostile reaction goes deep in the storehouse and comes out with vexation, irascibility, plus the heat of antagonism and malice.

Anger or rage hurts, and pains experienced in childhood do not magically evaporate as we grow older. They rumble and grumble around in us and often explode in quarrelsome, contentious, destructive behavior. We and those around us may become crabby, sullen, testy, and generally disagreeable. We may explode on innocent persons, in circumstances that astonish us. Once we explode, it is impossible to take our hurtful words or behavior away.

Why do we deny our feelings? It is as if we try to get away from them and ignore them. How we do love to call our anger or hostility by the name of frustration! We sanitize our hostility by claiming we have had a bad day. Most of all, we call our hostility *hurt*. Rather than troubling to work through feelings, we baptize them to make them holy. We disguise hostility and call it righteous indignation. It may well have more to do with being right (and how we do love to be right) than righteous indignation. Some persons disguise their hostility by proclaiming, "I am only telling you this for your own good." We can be so pious as we seek to baptize our feelings, rather than claim them. Hostility hurts us physically, emotionally, and spiritually. It especially hurts when we refuse to acknowledge it. Calling hostility by another name continues the process of being dishonest with ourselves. Are some people comfortable with their hostility? If they give up their hostility, what would be left? Is it possible they nurture, feed, and embrace their hostility? What would be gained if they gave it up?

When we get caught up in maladaptive behavior and patterns of hostility, we are trapped and unable to move forward. The persons we want to be in relationship with become the enemy. If we can be aware of our patterns of processing and learn the cause of our hostility, then we are open to becoming an ally, rather than an opponent, of our feelings. This will take considerable effort. We will be swimming against the current.

Repressed hostility accumulates, gathers force, becomes antagonistic and warlike. Our lack of hospitality, our being unfriendly and expressing enmity, are clues to others, but we may be unaware of what is taking place.

    The husband of one of my former clients had cheated on her from day one of their marriage. According to the culture in which her mother was reared, that was the way it was with men, and she might as well accept it. This emotional abuse went on for years. She had been referred to me by her physician, to deal with the stress in her life. It became evident that she was in a panic at having to deal with her long over-controlled hostility. Originally she had difficulty talking, sometimes freezing, unable to say a word. She had a solid Christian faith, but without any joy. She talked mostly about judgment, but was devoid of enthusiasm about grace or joy. I asked her if she remembered the story of Jesus cleansing the temple and she told the story to me. I reminded her that Jesus had stored up his feelings for a long time, but he used his stored-up hostility to right a tremendous wrong.

    Slowly she smiled, then began to laugh. She laughed until tears streamed down her face. Her next words startled me. "I can do that. If my Jesus could, then so can I." It was a permission-giving event for her. She laid her plans carefully. She had a long overdue confrontation with her husband. She told him that in marriage she had had the *worse* and she was ready to move on to the *better,* or he could move out the door! He chose to act as if she was joking. She was not. He continued to be disbelieving, but she was adamant. Finally they both came to therapy. It was difficult and exacting work, but both of them persevered. Eventually he admitted he wanted his wife to feel hurt as he had been hurt as a child. It was not rational, but it was an old powerless feeling that governed his adult functioning. Her mother also came in for a few sessions to repair the relationship with her daughter. His mother was dead, but we used some therapeutic interventions so that he could work out long-buried feelings concerning her. Occasionally I still hear from this client, who is seemingly free from old hostilities. She deals with feelings as they arise. On her last note she penned a postscript saying she had been asked to teach a class for young married adults: "I hope they too experience growth and find *their* truth that sets them free."

Anger, Rage, and Hostility

Anger, rage, and hostility are powerful emotions. As noted earlier, the most common initial reaction to any of these feelings is to label them as "hurt." Can we lift up our feelings, see what is underneath our initial reaction, and process our feelings? If we maintain we are hurt rather than acknowledge what we are really feeling, in all probability we will be more likely to receive sympathy. If we repeatedly tell our story to achieve sympathy, it reinforces our denial.

If we would be open to the possibility that we have these emotions, it would mean first-order change in our perceptions of self. It would mean facing our denial, and looking at the truths we have not wanted to face. I am told frequently by my clients that they do not express their anger because they are protecting others from the anger. They act as if their anger is so powerful, it would blow other people away. I find that most persons who say they are protecting others are in reality protecting themselves. But, of course, it sounds much more spiritual or religious to say we are protecting others—not ourselves. It is yet one more way of baptizing our actions so we appear spiritual.

In Miriam Greenspan's book *A New Approach to Women and Therapy* she admonishes that anger is the fuel we need to burn in the struggle to create a society without victims.[1] When we deny our own anger, we could be protecting ourselves by refusing to acknowledge the victimization in our world. The beautiful verse in Matthew 25 says, "Just as you did it to one of the least of these who are members of my family, you did it to me" (Mt. 25:40). Our responsibility to victims is not limited to our own family. Could we be deliberately hiding behind our so-called lack of anger feelings, in order to remain uninvolved?

The late Paul Tillich, that articulate theologian who states premises in words we wish were ours, said in one of his lectures (and I paraphrase) that God is present in the force that makes us

---

[1] Miriam Greenspan, *A New Approach to Women and Therapy* (Columbus, Ohio: McGraw-Hill, 1993).

restless. It is often our discomfort that moves us to action. If we cocoon ourselves in the comfort of not facing our anger, surrounded by persons who believe as we do, then we ignore the victims God calls us to help.

When we get caught up in maladaptive patters of rage and hostility, we become enemies of those with whom we want to be in relationship. Anger that becomes rage, and rage that becomes hostility, certainty control our lives in negative ways.

In those days when I lived out what I had been taught about anger by my parents, who were repeating what they had been taught in their families of origin. I repressed my anger, allowing it to become a powerful enemy of my own well-being. Gradually it took on the force of rage and hostility. When I blew up, I felt guilt, regret, and shame. I immediately apologized and began stuffing the anger I believed to be wrong.

Fury and Wrath

Fury and wrath are seen even less frequently than anger, rage, or hostility. Many people use the terms *anger, rage, hostility, fury,* or *wrath* interchangeably. This may well cause confusion in the minds of others. Some call any angerlike emotion by the name they heard most often from their families of origin, or from a coach, Sunday school teacher, or Scout leader.

As with anger and rage, many times persons who experience fury or wrath are experts at hiding what is going on inside themselves. Eventually they explode, and their resulting actions become the subject of newspaper and television reports. Unfortunately, only then do their feelings come to the attention of others. Many persons who exhibit these patterns of behavior have learned to be discreet in the presence of those who might see their behavior as deviant. They can be anti-social loners or put on carefully contrived facades. They are not particularly appealing as friends, nor do they often seek relationships. Rarely are they active in joining or being active in community events. They are described most often, after an event of assault or holding others hostage, as being unobtrusive neighbors who speak and go on without much conversation. They guard their privacy and have a tendency to mind their own business. When they "blow," all the internalized fury or wrath erupts in an overreaction.

Suppressed feelings gather momentum, surprising those associated with the fury-filled person previously. The feelings explosion may even surprise the person her- or himself.

Fury

We can compare fury to a raging storm that comes in speedily, with fierce winds. Fury is violent anger that is ready to blow, with tremendous turbulence and great fallout. It is hostility that has spawned into increased violent speech or actions. When I am in contact with vengeful persons, I immediately think of fury. If they are clients, I think of hospitalization. Often they are irrational, talking about events that at first appear to have recently happened, but turn out to be from the past. They hold grudges, refuse to look at options, and have the capacity for great destruction, sometimes despite an almost mousy facade. There is a hidden undercurrent that is often difficult to diagnose.

I well remember a young man, referred to me by his physician who called and told me he did not know what to do with him. I agreed to see him on an emergency basis. He arrived accompanied by his wife and parents. He was fragile, brittle, and ready to blow in all directions. I suggested that he looked weary, as if he were carrying a heavy burden. I asked about his sleep patterns, and as I suspected, he was sleeping poorly or not at all. He was living on cigarettes and black coffee, which is a lethal combination, adding to his desire to make somebody pay for his discomfort. After I spoke softly about my concern for him and his own weariness, he agreed to go to the hospital. He had not been there thirty minutes when he began to trash his room. Two orderlies intervened, but the violent anger had built up so much he hit both men, sending them to the emergency room. A long hospitalization helped him with his uncontrolled violence and raging fury. His intense emotions about past events had moved quickly from hostility to momentary insanity.

Wrath

Wrath comes through at first as deep indignation. It is a desperate desire to punish someone. Perhaps it is a desire to get even, as the person complains often about an old slight or hurt, which grows with each telling. Revenge is primary. People speak about wanting justice, needing justice to right a wrong. Old rage often brings on loss of self-control. Their frenzied actions may verge on madness. In conversation they are frequently insulting, demeaning the referring professional or family members who sent them for therapy. They ask angrily about a counselor's credentials. The wrathful person returns again and again to the necessity for revenge. This desire may evolve into an elaborate and complicated plan for how such revenge could be accomplished. Often such clients are quickly referred and hospitalized. While hospitalized they may put on a facade of compliance, continuing to talk about old hurts and slights, but without talking about revengeful plans to get even.

I have experienced some wrathful clients who seem to improve, only to backslide between appointments. More often they return to their tirade about how life has been exceedingly unjust to them and how they would punish whoever has done them wrong. When one wrathful client seemed on the verge of losing control, I would call time-out. Then he would take the big, soft pillow in my office and pulverize it. Pillows often had to be replaced, but it was a great advantage over destroying furniture. I had given him, in writing, a set of rules saying he was never to hit anything but the pillow. He read and signed my copy and kept a copy for himself. I suggested to him and his family that they purchase a punching bag in order for him to expel the feelings that swirled in his mind.

It is important to note that those who exhibit wrathful behavior need careful guidelines and a place to safely exhibit and expel their feelings of wrath. His punching bag at home was helpful as he worked out some old feelings. A course in a form of martial arts, where he learned to concentrate on a goal of discipline, not disaster, had meaning for him. His family told the referring doctor he was much improved and they terminated his counseling. The physician reported later they had moved out of the community. I hold no illusions he was cured, but he left feeling he had been heard, and that it was possible to vent his wrath on inanimate objects.

4

Other Negative Choices Concerning Anger

The natural response to angry behavior is the old "fight or flight" reaction. In the early days of civilization, it was workable. If you saw a saber-toothed tiger or a grizzly bear you had only two choices. You could pick up the biggest club you could find and hit the tiger or the grizzly bear into submission or death. Or you could run as fast as lightning and hopefully find a tree, where you could climb to safety.

Our world today does not lend itself to lashing out physically at every person or event that irritates, annoys, or angers us. Social norms, laws, and common sense limit our responses. Irate clients, unreasonable administrators, goof-off employees, or an overly tired child, not to mention a summons to the Internal Revenue Service, require us to react in an entirely different way, even if we momentarily fantasize about other responses.

In our society today many of our anger-associated feelings are nonspecific. We could have anger feelings about paying taxes in general, and these feelings erupt when we are questioned about our tax return. Years ago, when both of our children were very ill, our medical expenses were off the chart. The IRS audited our tax return. My husband went to the appointment armed with a thick file of medical bills, and an ingrained image of a "bean counter" who was out to get us. Imagine his surprise when a mature, smiling woman called his name. She checked his material, apologized for any inconvenience, and concluded by saying we were due a small refund.

The instinctive way to express our anger is to respond in an aggressive way when we are intimidated. Anger becomes a threat. One of the reasons anger is a threat is because when we are angry we often regress into a childlike ego state. It is as if we are without status, power, or even the ability to be heard in an adult world. Our voice changes, becoming louder for males and higher-pitched for females. Men frequently take on an aggressive, threatening stance. Females, much to their own disgust, have tears and a runny nose, which they believe takes away their power. Both behaviors are a threat to the opposite sex. Men are stronger, and some, but by no means all, resort to frightening women with an underlying threat of violence. Men tend to see women's tears as manipulative, calling it unfair fighting, and it can be for some females, but certainly not all.

Rationally, we understand that a difference of opinion is not a threat to our person. Irrationally, it may disquiet us. At some level it may threaten our basic beliefs or our well-earned reputation, or seem slanderous about those persons we care about. Internally, the anger behavior of others, may seem to call for us to make first-order changes, to examine our long-held values, and to remember feelings we thought were long forgotten or hidden away.

Outbursts of Anger

Instinctively, we respond to angry behavior in an aggressive way. Anger is a natural, adaptive response to any threat. When we are emotionally or physically wounded, it calls for powerful, aggressive feelings or actions. This allows us to defend ourselves when we attacked either verbally or physically. One of anger's basic functions is survival. Without it, the human race would be extinct. It was used to struggle against the elements of nature, and today it is a protection of human dignity. When we believe we are put down, ignored, ridiculed, or victimized, it is our anger that moves us to action.

However, we have choices other than hitting or hurling angry words. Problem-solving is never facilitated by name calling or shoving a fist in someone's face. Pouting may have worked to

Other Negative Choices Concerning Anger   33

get your own way in your family of origin, but as an adult there are better ways. It is difficult (to be hones, it is impossible) to avoid events or persons who enrage us—sometimes by their presence, sometimes by their absence. Many of us know only two ways of handling anger or rage: aggression or supression. Such limited choices give a bad name to any angry feelings, and accomplish little.

Destructive anger is a big, often unvoiced fear. Will I hurt someone with my anger? Will that person hurt me? What if I really let myself go? Must I keep the demon within me contained and under rigid control? It is so easy to view all relationships in terms of cause and effect. If I am angry, someone caused me to be angry. If another person who is in relationship to me is angry, then I must be to blame. How did I cause this anger? I must be responsible for what they are feeling. Ruminating can set up more angry feelings, leading to irresponsible actions.

Outbursts of anger are never thought through. Usually they are a primitive or a childlike expression of feelings. They reflect a desire to get even or to "show someone" that the angry person can't be walked on.

Anger can be very destructive when we insist on always being right, or take the stance that every time we are angry someone else is to blame. Rage may linger because we do not have all the facts, or because being right is more important than anything else, even having a relationship. The longer we wait to look at the big picture of our rage, the easier it is to assess blame. Issues are lost. Pain and disillusion remain. Truth is elusive and difficult to discern without adequate calm and thoughtful dialogue.

Such angry outbursts may happen anywhere. Last week I heard a virtual storm of negative and even curse words heaped on a pharmacy employee. because the pharmacy could not refill a prescription for a strong pain medication without a written prescription from the physician. The customer went into a rage, saying, "We were not required to have this in the state we moved from. This is a backward place to live. I want to see the manager." The employee called the pharmacist, who left his tasks and came out to talk with the angry person, who by now was even more unreasonable. The pharmacist brought out the statute book detailing the filling of narcotic prescriptions. Far from being appeased, the customer stormed through the store loudly declaring he would never return. One person who had waited very patiently during the outburst quietly said, "That sounds like good news to me." The outburst accomplished absolutely nothing. It wasted the time of the six persons waiting, the pharmacist, and the employee, and created an atmosphere of wrath.

Repressing Anger

Repression is keeping down or holding back. It is a control so strict and severe it prevents natural expression or development. Ideas painful to the conscious mind are pushed down into the subconscious. To quell or crush these feelings stops a natural flow, but after a while the subduing of emotion seems normal. Suppressed ideas and impulses take energy to bring into consciousness. It can be done, but it will take effort. Many of us are so fearful of our anger we try to avoid it at all costs. When it does come up we try to ignore it, hoping it will go away. Of course it does not go away. To repeatedly repress anger causes it to go underground, and it often recycles and comes out as depression or physical illness. Repression is, of course, a form of denial, and a dangerous way of dealing with anger. The emotion is only temporarily shelved. Yet many of us learned this method in our families of origin. But if we learned, it we can unlearn it. Repressed anger can become very bitter and powerful. Without our knowledge it festers and grows. Then it emerges out of our immediate control. Thus, we convince ourselves we are free of anger. Or as my friend who was late for lunch said, "I have conquered my anger," when in reality it was just suppressed.

Repressed anger has such an impact on our well-being that a standard question I use in intake interviews is, "What do you do with your anger?" Time after time, after much thought, clients respond, "I'm not sure. I guess I never get angry." It is a vital clue that the client is repressing anger. Unfortunately, many times people considered religious are the worst offenders. They have assumed it is unchristian to acknowledge anger, but actually, repression of anger does not mix well with Christianity.

It is not unusual for a client to come to counseling seeking help to be more patient with a spouse, sibling, or child. The client denies anger, stating the desire to be a good spouse, sibling, or parent. It takes some time to build enough trust for the client to admit, often tearfully, their fear of rejection if they say what they truly feel about a loved one. I remember a female client who was dowdy, sweet, subservient, and ever so patient. She had married an older man with three children who were totally out of control. His first wife had been killed in an accident, and he had been so involved with his grief that he elicited a promise from his bride-to-be that she would never be angry with his children. The children figuratively held their stepmother hostage. Their behavior was impossible. She cried and told me how she prayed for patience. I asked her why she did not pray for courage. I suggested she talk with friends who had known the family before the death of the mother. She was surprised to learn the children had been well behaved. She decided she was a failure and was ready to leave. I suggested, since she was leaving anyway, she should tell the children and her husband exactly how she felt. She got them all together and gave them fourteen months' worth of anger and frustration. She cited the lack of support from her husband, the unreasonable demands of the children, how she cleaned the house only to have it in shambles minutes later, and the total lack of appreciation for meals fixed or errands run. She talked until she was hoarse, then declared she was sick and tired of trying to be patient, and that she would be leaving immediately. She was amazed when with one voice they begged her to stay. She said, "Why?" And they told her for the first time she seemed like a real person. Becoming a functioning family, as well as having a workable marriage, did not happen overnight. I worked with them for over two years while he and the children worked out their anger over the death of his first wife and their mother, and discovered impatience as a virtue.

Repressed anger is not healthy. A catharsis can help in healing damaged emotions. In Bill Moyers's book *Healing and the Mind* he says, "So a part of health is letting these true emotions of grief and sorrow and anger and fear work their way through to catharsis."[1] Moyers asks Candace Pert, Ph.D., a visiting professor at the Center for Molecular and Behavioral Neuroscience at Rutgers University, if repressing emotions is bad for us. She states,

---

[1] Bill Moyers, *Healing and the Mind* (New York: Doubleday and Co., 1993), 191.

"It appears that suppression of grief, and suppression of anger, in particular is associated with an increased incidence of breast cancer in women."[2] Forgetting and repression are not the same. I forget where I left my car keys. and have to look and look until I run across them. If we repress something it is out of our conscious mind, but not out of our unconscious. We can get so adept at repressing our emotions that it may take professional help to raise them to the conscious level. It is well worth the effort and helps us become all that we are meant to be.

Passive-Aggressive Anger

Passive-aggression is another way of hiding from our own anger. Such aggression is always expressed indirectly. The passive-aggressive person always sees him- or herself as acted upon, never the actor, so how can he or she be blamed? It is a safe way of being aggressive without being accountable for it. Humor is another favorite way of expressing anger without being responsible. If you take umbrage at the humor, the person, looking crestfallen, says, "Can't you take a joke? I was only kidding. What's the matter with you?"

Passive-aggression is a neat, bloodless way of never being responsible, always placing the blame on someone else. Substance abusers frequently blame the alcohol that *made them* say all those nasty remarks they never would have said if they had been sober. It is a common pattern for alcoholics to swallow their anger, then take a drink to wash the anger down. Thus when the angry words are spoken, blame is put on the booze. Once again the angry person is acted upon, but is never the actor.

Not surprisingly, this is the method most often used by Christians to deal with their anger. It was the way I was taught both by experience and example. Remember: "Nice people do not get angry." "Christians do not get angry." "Young ladies do not get angry." Why can't I just go on with these maxims I have been taught all my life? If it were workable, I would. But it is neither honest nor healthy. Each time I follow the "nice people do not get angry" theory, I find I still have to do something with

---

[2]Ibid.

my anger. I have been taught not to express or release it, so that leaves repressing my anger. I stick it inside, hold it back, and work to keep it down. Since God made me human (and it is human to forget that and try to be divine), a day always comes when my repressed anger will not stay down. Some small thing will cause an avalanche of anger. When I finally realized that a change in my pattern of dealing with anger was long overdue, it was a healthy change in my life.

Torrents of anger often spill from those described as someone "who never gets angry," always so "nice" and never one to raise the voice, until that day when the dam breaks and a cyclone of words swirls out, inundating all those in the vicinity. Or as I described in the first chapter, I would erupt like Mount St. Helens. Then if I were to retain my "nice" image I had to backtrack and begin once again to stockpile my anger for the next blow, whether it be for two weeks or two years. It was an unproductive way of dealing with the gift of anger. Dealing with the gift of anger in a a passive-aggressive way is also unproductive, as many times the person you are angry with does not receive your sarcasm or know it is directed at them. Working with one client who just could not accept that he was passive-aggressive, I asked if I could illustrate by using actual examples. When he agreed, I asked if he remembered saying to me that I was only nice to him because I was paid to be nice to him. He laughed a forced kind of laugh and said he didn't mean anything. Then I asked, "Why did you say it if you did not mean it?" Then he admitted he was angry because he had to be in therapy.

I responded, "Had to be in therapy?" He hemmed and hawed and finally said he was coerced into coming for therapy by his boss, who said he had to learn not to zing people with his anger. Customers had reported him and asked not to work with him when they came next time. After questioning, the client admitted that the customers may have been upset because he felt his time was as important as that of the clients and that they ought to adhere to his schedule. Since he was an only child of indulgent er parents, he thought life should go his way. I suggested he was living in a fantasy world if he believed he would always get his own way. We worked for weeks on a reality orientation where he brought in a week's worth of anger and we talked about how he could appropriately use his anger. It was not easy for him to change, and every now and then he slipped back in his old pattern of zinging those who did not please him. One day he said, "I've got it. Being passive-aggressive is like going swimming, but never getting in the water. No one knows what is going on, you feel uncomfortable, and everyone has a good time but you." I smiled and said, "Yes, is that the way you want to live?"

Frequently humor is used to convey passive-aggressive anger. You can avoid responsibility for your anger by saying, "I was just teasing; can't you take a joke?" This puts the onus on the other person, as if he or she is responsible. I am remembering a couple I had in marriage counseling who were both passive-aggressive. As they were trying to schedule an appointment to come in again, he became impatient with her. He worked two jobs while she was not employed, and he felt her garden club meeting was not important. She accused him of making fun of her. He shouted, "You set the appointment. I'll change my other commitments." He laughed a gallows laugh. She began to cry, making mewing noises about how she was always the one who had to give in, and he was the one who always won. Since this looked to be a repeat of many of their previous disagreements, I arbitrarily set the appointment a week away. The next week she reported that she had cried all the way home and had retaliated by not doing any laundry all week. I asked each of them what they had gained from their behavior. He said, "I got some new underwear." They both tittered, and I suggested we talk about what was underneath their tittering. After twenty-four years of marriage, they had never learned to communicate effectively. They prided themselves on never arguing, but their cold war would erupt every now and then. I suggested that an honest dialogue would accomplish far more than this kind of game-playing. It took time to learn communication skills and not slip back into the nonproductive, passive-aggressive ways they knew so well.

I once worked with a senior pastor who was adept at pushing duties on me that were not in my job description as minister of education. He always cloaked these requests in such a way that it took a while to catch on to what was happening. Before long I was asked to do liturgy for two services, "since my voice was clearer for the radio and the taping for the shut-in ministry," than the voice of the staff member who usually did the liturgy. Then gradually I was assigned more tasks that had no connection with the education program of this large church. When I was asked to assume hospital visitation two days a week, I had had my limit. I said I could not do this task and keep up my regular work. He assumed a hurt look, saying, "But Doris, I just wanted to give you a greater exposure to the congregation." The hurt-little-boy look had worked for him, getting others to do tasks in such a way they thought it was an honor, not realizing how they had been manipulated. It was a way of not being direct and making the underling seem to be an angry, ungrateful employee. The employer remained passive-aggressive and ever so nice, so I sought another position.

Silence may well be the cruelest form of anger avoidance. Silent anger is often used effectively to "even the score" with another person. This anger can be very subtle and leave the other person feeling powerless. No angry words are expressed, no threats, nothing to have to apologize about. Silent anger is another form of passive-aggressive behavior. This is a very controlling form of anger. One client described his wife as "going silent on me." Then he explained he would play "twenty questions" to try to elicit what was wrong with her. He would ask if she had a headache, was there a problem with the children, had things gone badly at work and so on. No response. After a while his own anger would rise as he felt powerless, while she just sat there silently. Often people who use passive-aggressive methods to avoid anger are attracted to those who are more aware of their own feelings. They want others to work to make the relationship viable, then if anything goes wrong they can blame the other person. If you let your feelings be known, then you must be responsible for them.

Procrastination is another way of being passive-aggressive. This is a lazy form of rebellion, but again without having to take the responsibility. If I don't do it, then no one can complain I did not do it right. It is easy to procrastinate without raising your voice or raising a finger. You just do nothing. My, how controlling it is, especially when others are waiting for you to do your part so that they can do their part. It is a passive-aggressive way of telling others: Wait for me; I am important. You are not. What power, from a passive act! Or you may be angry with a spouse, a parent, or a sibling, so you make them wait until you finally push aside your procrastination and "do them a favor" by doing what you were supposed to be doing all along. Control becomes the issue, and the passive aggressive person excels in control.

Other forms of passive-aggressive behavior can be found when work is done in a sloppy way. You do the bare minimum, and no more. One man told me that if he acted as if he could not do the yard tasks assigned to him by his father, but just piddled along, then his dad would eventually come and help him finish the assigned work. It is a way of "showing" the boss or the parent, without open rebellion. Thus you are never responsible for your actions. Forgetting is yet another way of being passive with anger. Gosh, I forgot; everyone forgets, don't they? This is another way of saying that the agenda of others is not important. Being preoccupied and set apart from the family or a committee can communicate that what the others are about is not of interest. Grumbling may be a passive way of dealing with feelings of anger, and such feelings may be the root of laziness. It is a passive way of dealing with the expectations of others, hoping they will leave you alone. So the anger is never dealt with properly, and it remains inside until it blows others over.

Thanks, I Needed That!

How odd are the bits and pieces of information we store in the attic of our minds. I try to recall the name of the person who just came into the room. The face is familiar, but the more I search for the name, the more elusive it becomes. As we begin to converse, the Mississippi accent triggers my memory and the name is there as if it had never left. Jingles, commercials, and other trivia are usually quite easily recalled. Perhaps, it is the repetition, the rhyming, the nonsensical words, or sometimes the poor grammar that cause these to be fixed in the crevices of our minds. As we age we have more to scroll through to find a particular memory. I suppose there is a lesson to be found in what we retain and what is more difficult to retrieve. Or it could be we have a made a decision along the way that we can't remember it all.

I can clearly recall the old slapstick routine where one hapless person is hit in the face with a meringue pie. Scraping the gobs of goo off his face, he says, "Thanks, I needed that!" This routine moved to the world of advertising where it was co-opted to sell a product. It also became a phrase that was bandied about whenever anyone felt unfairly judged or accused. Was it not also a passive-aggressive way of expressing anger, without having to be responsible for the feeling? To say "thanks" for getting hit in the face with a gooey pie, which messed up their clothing as well as their face and hair, makes no sense at all, Yet it continues to happen in our society, and we continue to let it happen. Why? Is this a way of hiding our real feelings, of playing the game of business, or is it self-protection?

Do we love ourselves so little we think we ought to be misused by others? Are we too cowardly to stand up for ourselves? Do we feel we have no right to disagree even when we are being ridiculed? Or perhaps we have such a reservoir of feelings that we are afraid to tap into that deep, dark swamp of emotions. Are you afraid you might hurt someone, or are you the one you are protecting? We have an exaggerated idea of our own power, assuming we are powerful enough to blow someone away. But the truth sets us free, and it is worth some bits and pieces of anxiety for this to happen.

Anger is a natural reaction to frustration. We feel anger when it seems to us we are rejected and we feel put down and less than human. This creates a feeling of being powerless. We may ruminate, wondering over and over why this has happened, and why it has happened to *me*. We have a feeling of deprivation— why me? As one of my adolescent clients phrases it, "Life sucks!" We feel as if (and say), "Life is not fair," and of course it isn't. And where did we read it was going to be? Is this found in chapter 1, verse 7 of the book of *Entitlements?* If we are using that for our Bible, we are in dire need of a new translation. Anger is a legitimate emotion and gives various clues to what is wrong in our life. It may be a sign of unresolved conflict, a conflict that we need to follow scriptural injunction to resolve. Following Jesus' words on conflict resolution in Matthew 18:15–17, we need to pray about the conflict, to get as clear a picture as possible of what caused the conflict and what *needs to be done to resolve it.* Then we go and talk to the person with whom we had the conflict. If this does not resolve it, then take a trusted, level-headed friend with you to try again to resolve the conflict. The conflict is a warning that things need to be changed. Sometimes, what needs to be changed is us. The willingness to confront conflict is a healthy way to resolve the issue. The "Thanks, I needed that" school of reacting is a prime way to create resentment or even bitterness.

Long-standing anger may be the result of grief that has never been worked through. Grief will not go away by itself. It may go underground and cause sleepless nights. It certainly can cause depression. It may bring gastric upsets, a series of headaches, and a general malaise. We grieve over the loss of any person or anything that has meaning for us. One can grieve over a forced retirement, a divorce, a broken engagement, not getting into the graduate school of our choice, or the death of close family members and friends. We so often see grief as only sadness, and it is that, but the power underlying the sadness is the anger concerning not getting our way, as well as the loss of control that death brings home to us.

Destructive Anger

Destructive anger is the big, often unvoiced fear of almost everyone. What happens if I really let myself go? Would I hurt someone seriously? What kind of a demon do I have in me that I think is contained only if I keep myself under rigid control?

Anger can be destructive when we insist on being right, or because it feels good to have someone to blame. Frequently anger lingers because we do not have all the facts, and as it lingers it festers. Being right becomes more important than having a relationship. As time goes by it becomes more difficult to look at issues, and easier to assess blame. The issues are lost, but the pain and disillusionment remain. If your self-esteem depends on always being right, then reconciliation is not sought. Even if you are right, is it worth losing a relationship? Being right can be very lonely, and in the big picture what does it matter after all?

It just might go under the heading, "Don't sweat the small stuff!" And in the final analysis, isn't it all small stuff?

Hitting another human being is inexcusable. Hitting a child or a weaker person because we are enraged is criminal. An old adage that is blatantly false is: "Spare the rod, and spoil the child." Trust that is violated at an early age creates an inability to trust that can last a lifetime. Since trust is the foundation of a workable marriage, the inability to trust leads to quarrels, more distrust, communication problems, frequent separations, and at times divorce.

There is much that needs to be said and done concerning destructive anger. Violence depicted by the news media, brutality acted out in our movies, senseless and almost casual killing splashed across our TV screens—these are accepted by us to the tune of billions of dollars in advertising, plus billions more spent on "hit" movies that glorify violence and destruction. Not only do they make money, but also they entertain the masses. Is this not reminiscent of the Christians being tossed to the lions to entertain the rich Romans? Are we content to subscribe to this not only with our money but with the impressionable minds and psyches of our children?

Abusive Anger

Rape, child abuse, spouse abuse, and abuse of the elderly are telling reasons to fear anger behavior that destroys and devalues persons. To walk away from, ignore, or remain silent upon witnessing such devastating events is unconscionable. It is easy to persuade ourselves that it is not our business; but of course that excuse will not wash, especially when we face ourselves. Molested children, often violated by a family member or friend of the family, wonder how they can trust God, whom they cannot see, since adults whom they can see are not to be trusted.

Such rage experienced in childhood only festers and grows. Swallowed rage creates voiceless victims, only to have such rage become a part of them, which is then inappropriately dumped on other people. They may even pride themselves on being honest, not realizing how cruel they are. The child who has been abused becomes a harsh and demanding parent. It is evident once again when a child, as an adult, becomes the caregiver for an aging parent. It is not easy to be calm with a parent with Alzheimer's disease, who has lost her memory, her reasoning ability, and likely the control of her bladder and bowels. Unfortunately I see many adult children who have made a promise to an aging relative that they will never put the relative in a nursing home (which, by the way, is not the worst-case scenario for aging parents). Such a promise may be good in theory, but day-to-day care giving is confining and it is easy to grow weary, disgusted, or depressed. Elder abuse is the fastest growing kind of abuse in our culture today. Sometimes it's a case of an adult who was abused as a child and has carried wrath inside. Finally, the abused becomes the abuser, as the parent grows dependent on the child.

In some cultures adults feel they have a God-given right to abuse their children. (In reality all children have a right to be treated as loved individuals.) Too many times a spanking becomes a beating. A client who had been spanked as a child spanked her own child. How appalled she was to discover her child playing with her dolls and spanking them. When she asked, "Why?" the child responded, "Mommies do not have to have a reason to spank." The abused becomes the abuser. My client talked with me about other ways to discipline her child. As my client changed behavior, so did her daughter as she played with her dolls.

Destructive behaviors are often in relationships between men and women. Traditionally, women are fundamentally identified with their own bodies. "Men are their brains, women are their bodies." I heartily dislike such statements. Unfortunately, some men see it as their prerogative to make use of a woman's body with or without her consent. Rape and the threat of rape is the most insidious form of male domination. Rape is never a crime of passion. Rape is an act of aggression! Broken down to its basics, it is the taking of what a man wants, even when it is not his to take. This behavior exemplifies the actions of a two-year-old: "I want what I want, when I want it," without a moral qualm.

Rape is violence. Rape is a chargeable offense. But untold numbers of females are raped and no charges are filed because of the fear of reprisals or publicity. Even newspaper and TV reports refer to the victim's being out late at night, even when she has just left her place of employment, as if the victim had incited the rape. The previous sexual history of the woman can be introduced in a court of law in some states, but rarely the sexual acts of the perpetrator unless he was convicted. Is it any wonder that clients who have been raped have difficulty dealing with the anger and rage surrounding such happenings? Such rage can preclude a workable relationship with any male until the rage is dealt with therapeutically.

Not all men accused of rape are guilty. A man can be a scapegoat of circumstances. As with other crimes, the outcome of guilt or innocence alone may be misleading, for the accusation alone brings a stigma. The charge is newsworthy. If the accused is deemed innocent, or if a charge is dropped, such news is often put on the inside pages. Need we wonder at the anger and rage that builds in those unjustly accused? When this happens, some men decide never to trust any female, and if they marry, their trust level is so low they may constantly accuse and belittle the wife. It may not stop there, for children learn distrust and paranoia firsthand. Such distrust may lead to abuse of spouse or children—and preclude seeking help.

Most people abhor violence, especially to women and children, and yet such abuse continues. More and more shelters for abused women and children are being built because of a growing need for them. Even more horrifying is the death rate of wives, girlfriends, and lovers, plus the incredible number of infants and small children who are beaten, shaken, choked, cut, burned, and/or mutilated. This crime of rage may seem spontaneous, but in reality it has grown over the years until it takes over the person completely. The denial afterward is usually accompanied by sobbing and the blaming of other persons or events, which cannot bring back a shattered life. Such persons are in serious need of long-term, in-depth psychotherapy. Children and women who have been abused and through the grace of God are still alive, cannot quickly achieve forgiveness. They need to value themselves enough to look within and work out the myriad issues that accompany such abuse. The abused may think the abuse is her own fault, as the abuser tells the victim, "I wouldn't have hurt you, but you asked for it. It's all your fault."

Many victims accept such a concept. Victims need a caring person to encourage them to seek needed help. Low self-esteem may well be the trademark of victims, and abuse lowers self-esteem dramatically.

Abuse comes in many forms, some of it quite subtle. Some abusers, both men and women, are proud of the fact that they have never laid a hand on their children or spouses. But the erosion of another's ego strength, over time, is serious abuse. When a person feels he can never do anything right, that whatever he does turns out wrong, or that there is no use in trying anymore, this is as crippling as physical abuse. I frequently overhear conversations in restaurants, groceries, or malls in which children are put down so completely I wonder how they will recover. All parents lose patience, but this not an excuse for unkind remarks. I see clients who are still struggling with parental remarks such as, "You're just like your grandpa" or "You will never amount to anything" or "You need to learn how to please a man, for you are not pretty enough to get a man otherwise." Why do parents feel they have a right, perhaps even a God-given right, to abuse their children? Children have a right to be treated with the same respect due any person.

The abused's becoming an abuse is a frequent occurrence. The child who has been abused becomes a harsh and demanding parent, and if put into a caretaking role with the parent, they may turn on the elderly parent. As noted earlier, some adult children have been "guilted" into the care-giving role by a promise elicited from a parent begging the adult child to never place the parent in a retirement or nursing home. Others are trapped by, "What will people say?" or "Everyone will think I don't love my mom or dad," or "How could you do that to your aunt or uncle?" Remember that people do not always engage their brain before they speak. Their main concern may be themselves, and what is going to happen when they no longer can care for themselves.

Abuse is a chargeable offense, whether the abuse involves a child, spouse, or older person. There is no excuse for abuse! The abuser may recognize the low self-esteem of the victim, or know the person is weaker, and as a bully sees the person as someone he or she can exploit. There are self-help groups to work with victims who want to leave victimhood behind forever.

Other Negative Choices Concerning Anger   47

Spouse abuse centers are listed in the Yellow Pages in every town and city. But listings can be confusing. It is advisable to look up such numbers ahead of time if you suspect you many need them. In some cities shelters may be listed under "spouse abuse"; in other cities the listings are under "associations." In addition, colleges and universities have specially trained persons to help deal with abuse or "date rape." Your pastor can also be of assistance when you need confidential help. If your church is fortunate enough to have a counseling center, make use of it for professional help and an understanding ear.

A number of organizations work with perpetrators of abuse. The decision to seek help may be motivated by the court, an attorney, a family member, or perhaps an attempt to avoid a jail term. It is very difficult for an abuser to accept blame, when he or she has always blamed someone else. The rapist cries, "She wanted it! I know she wanted me to take her." Counseling centers, mental health clinics, and hospitals offer twelve-step programs for sexual offenders. Substance abuse may accelerate problems such as sexual violence and loss of control. Addiction issues necessitate professional help. Adult children of an addicted parent exhibit certain characteristics. Alcoholics Anonymous and Al-Anon are free groups working with those addicted to alcohol or other substances, and to work with family members who may enable alcoholic behavior. Also, many communities have groups for Adult Children of Alcoholics (ACOA). Such groups are listed in the phone book. Some major cities and some counties have chapters of Adults Molested as Children (AMAC), which focus on the severe dysfunction caused by abuse by a trusted parent or caregiver. Of necessity these persons had to swallow rage when they were voiceless victims, but this rage may come out inappropriately as they dump their anger on others, believing they are being honest. In reality they are fearful of confronting their abusers, so they confront others. Being a friend to or married to a person who has been abused calls for fortitude, patience, and endurance. Even after therapy, they may continue to test to see if you really still love them.

We fear destructive anger so much that we do not wish to see or acknowledge it. We don't want to get involved. In the story of the good Samaritan, I read of the good, nice, religious persons who did not want to get involved. The priest saw the beaten man and decided to walk on the other side of the road. I'm sure he rationalized that he was too busy, and besides he had important work to do. Or the Levite, who passed by the robbed and beaten man, may have thought, "Why is this my responsibility? Why am I expected to get involved?" Perhaps he even echoed words uttered by Cain in Genesis: "Am I my brother's keeper?" But the Samaritan, usually avoided by the *good people,* saw the battered and bruised man, and he had compassion. What a beautiful word. What a beautiful act. The Samaritan went to the man and bound up his wounds, poured on the victim's wounds oil and wine from his own meager supply, placed him on his own beast, and brought him to the inn. He gave the innkeeper money to take care of the man, and promised to return and pay any additional charges. He had compassion, and he was willing to get involved. And Jesus said, "Go and do likewise."

5

Making Positive Choices about Our Anger

Frederick Buechner, in his book *The Longing for Home,* writes,

> Happiness comes when things are going our way, which makes it only a forerunner to the unhappiness that inevitably follows when things stop going our way, as in the end they will stop for all of us. Joy, on the other hand, does not come because something is happening or not happening but every once in a while rises up out of simply being alive, or being a part of the terror as well as the fathomless richness of the world that God has made.[1]

We cannot know a world without anger. To long for that is to long for a fantasy world. Anger, rage, and hostility are a very real part of our world. We do not have to be controlled by these emotions, but we can channel them to be used for our own good, and for the good of others. Anger has many functions. It gives us the energy to fight injustice and prejudice, and the needed adrenaline to act. And there are a number of positive choices we can make that enable us to live out God's gift of anger in a productive way.

---

[1] Frederick Buechner, *The Longing for Home: Reflections at Midlife* (San Francisco: HarperSanFrancisco, 1996), 128.

Expressing My Anger

We have all had the misfortune to know one or more persons trained in the "let it all hang out" school of anger. This behavior could have been learned from parents or friends. In the late sixties and early seventies we heard much about "doing your own thing." This was also the time period when the commercials declared, "You only go around once, so go with gusto," or "Go ahead, you're worth it." Of course such television ads sold goods, and they were easy for some to internalize and believe. It was also the time when confession was seen as purging and good for the soul, often with no regard for whom they wounded.

I remember one client who confessed to his wife about a casual affair he'd had while on business in another country. They called for an appointment with me when he could not believe how angry his wife was over his confession. In our first conjoint session he admitted his surprise that his wife did not feel as free and relaxed about the subject as he did. He said plaintively, "I was honest with her. What more does she want from me? His so-called honesty took the burden from him, but laid it squarely on her heart. They spent many sessions working on a marriage they both wanted to keep and make strong. It was long and tedious work looking at the integrity of anger, learning to listen to each other, and seeing how "your right to swing your fist ends where my nose begins."

There are many ways to express anger without doing harm to another. Talking about anger is most important in purging your feelings, but sometimes you have to hold onto feelings until you reach an appropriate person or persons to whom to express your anger. When I was a department head in a hospital, I was asked to see a dying employee. When I went to the patient unit, I was stopped by an acquaintance who was there with her comatose, terminally ill mother. She asked me to come in and have a prayer with her mother and her siblings, and I was glad to do so. When I finished, they began to make plans for their mother's funeral. I asked them to step out into the hall and then asked if they knew that hearing is often the last sense to go with the comatose. I suggested they might want to make such plans out of the possible hearing of their mother. I went on to see the employee I came to see and returned by the same route to the elevator. To my chagrin, I could hear the family still planning their mom's funeral as they stood around her bed. I was so angry at their insensitivity. I returned to my office, grateful I did not have a solo practice and had professional colleagues to whom I could vent. It did not change the family's lack of sensitivity, but it was helpful to dialogue with my coworkers and tell them what had happened. My colleagues shared my frustration and my anger, and my feelings slowly dissipated.

Anger is not always expressed verbally. Nonverbal expressions of anger can include a stern look (sometimes called a parental look), a slam of a door, a cold glare, ignoring or not talking to a person, or crying. After all, about half of our communication is nonverbal. Imagination dictates how we express anger in a nonverbal way. Caution needs to be exercised that we do not express anger in a way that asserts our superiority. If we do, others feel defensive and build up resentment that often causes the next disagreement. Be aware that you have a reason for expressing anger, other than just being cross or getting even. Plotting to get even creates a crucible that can create anger and lay the groundwork for the next argument. Expressing anger needs the right time and the right setting. To wait until someone is ready to walk out the door and then dump anger on him or her is inappropriate, and could be dangerous. Driving with anger causes inattention leading to accidents. Learn when and how to share angry feelings. How unfair it is when an employer tells an employee on Friday afternoon, "I want to see you in my office first thing Monday morning." How much better to either tell the person what's wrong right then, or to wait until Monday morning to mention it at all, rather than having the employee "stew" over the entire weekend.

One form of showing anger involves how we drive our vehicles. A new phrase has evolved to explain this way of inappropriately expressing anger: "road rage." We know that driving and alcohol do not mix, and we are painfully learning that anger and driving do not mix. More and more persons are expressing aggression when they get behind the wheel. The larger vans, panel trucks, sport utility vehicles, fast and flashy sports cars, and even sluggish older-model cars are all used in this demolition derby during the daily commute. Courtesy seems to be unknown. Driving the speed limit results in being passed by, it seems, everyone on the road. Horns honk aggressively if one is in the passing lane doing the maximum speed. Angry gestures are rudely thrown to any who impede drivers' way, while lanes are switched without signaling. Parking garages can be hotbeds of hostility. Most of us have empathy with driving around and around a high-rise garage and passing several places where persons have ensconced themselves in two spaces, while you have none. But does it really change behavior to leave an angry note on the windshield of the offending vehicle? I recently noted angry words being exchanged by two men in a church parking lot because one declared his door was damaged by the door of the neighboring car. Unfortunately, it happens to all of us, but how do we express it in healthy ways?

Since we cannot control the behavior of others, we need to try to avoid unnecessary provocation of the anger of others. We can make a resolution to not tailgate. If you hit a car in the rear, almost always you are charged. As much as you may want to drive in the passing lane, many states have laws to keep passing lanes clear. We can allow more time for each trip we take. What do we do with the five minutes we save by recklessly passing every car on the road? We can dim our high beam headlights, and only use our horn to avoid accidents. And we can stay out of our vehicles when we are angry. Taking a walk allows us to think and feel without endangering others, and is a good way of dissipating anger, while making a decision to postpone our anger. If someone lights your fuse just as you are leaving for your commute, try setting a time to dialogue at a later time. This gives you time to organize your thoughts and deal with issues rather than personalities. It also gives you time to think about why you are feeling so much anger about this particular issue.

Releasing My Anger

Released anger is not the same as repressed anger, discussed in the previous chapter. Releasing anger is a conscious decision to let go of that which you no longer have to keep repressed or pushed down. You let go of what you no longer need. Of course, we do not have the ability to release anger until we learn to work at the art of expressing our anger. When we gain the clarity to look deep within ourselves and acknowledge our anger, painful as that my be, then we can release it as we no longer need to hold on to that which is not useful. Sometimes we will just have to dismiss our anger knowing that we cannot change people, and we surely can not pick apples from orange trees. I overheard a person describe a neighbor as having an even disposition—it was always nasty. It may be hard to admit that we have some very difficult persons in our lives, and some of them are even related to us. It's even harder to admit that it may be us whom others find difficult.

Much more has been written about expressing anger than about releasing anger. Why beat your head against a brick wall, if you know nothing will change? It is unfortunate to have a supervisor or a coach who will never admit when he is wrong. When this happens we have a choice to make. I may not like the choices I have, but I do have choices. If I find my digestion is upset, or I have an increasing number of tension headaches, or I am having sleepless nights, then quitting the job or leaving the team may be my best choice, even though it is unfair to have to do so. It may not be fair to have to take a position that pays less or to leave a team that is playing well, but peace of mind can be "a pearl of great price." In an ideal world the coach would be fired or the supervisor would be sent for remedial training in how to work with employees. Since I live in a real world, my task is to release my anger, then get on with living my life. Once I accept that people who are taking away my peace of mind have no thought of changing, I accept that if I want things to be better in my life, it is up to me to initiate change.

Dismissing anger may seem hard to do. Sometimes we desire to hold onto our anger, hoping someone will fix it for us. It will not happen. It is our feeling, and it is ours to deal with. Or we could decide to blast someone with our anger, often a less powerful person, in order to help us feel powerful. It becomes a game of "teeter-totter," in which I knock you down and I go up, but quickly that is reversed and I am down. Such "scapegoating" is cowardly and does not achieve the desired results. The choice is ours. A brisk walk helps to clear the mind and helps it open to options not previously considered. Swimming, bowling, or playing tennis or golf clears our thinking and allows us to switch from how we have been wronged to what we can do. Talking with a good friend can bring a new perspective, or writing down our complaints helps us to a clearer vision.

Creative imagery can be most helpful as we try to release our feelings. Clients teach me much. In working with a man who had great difficulty releasing his anger, I suggested creative imagery. After a while he was really creative. In one session he told me of a very hard-to-work-with contractor. The client needed to finish the job both for his reputation and for financial considerations. He said he imaged sucking up this contractor in a huge, industrial-size vacuum cleaner, and he burst into laughter even as he told me. He said this image helped him to ignore the undesirable person and concentrate on doing his work.

In marriage it is even more difficult to release our anger appropriately. The people we love the most also have the greatest capacity for raising angry feelings in us. Living so intimately with a person creates very intense feelings. When my husband and I had a disagreement it was so easy for each of us to feel we were so right. This is why we usually agreed to make an appointment to talk about it later at a mutually acceptable time. (The subject of timing is discussed more fully later in this chapter.)

This gave us both time to be more objective. It was also more honest and fair, as I was more facile with words and it gave him an opportunity to marshal his thoughts. Most importantly, it gave each of us time to pray. It is impossible to be pig-headed or self-important when you dialogue with God. After our thinking and praying, it was surprising how much we agreed, despite our earlier disagreement. It took practice and patience to learn to release anger with the man I loved. Sometimes we had to look and see why we were so angry. Had it brought up old tapes from our families of origin, or old prejudices, or had we stepped on the toe of a tradition, unbeknownst to us? In the beginning we tripped over some regional differences or "sacred cows" we did not know were sacred. As we learned to communicate better, we learned to love more, and to be freer in releasing our feelings.

The idea of being able to release anger can be confusing. What I hear most often is, "I can't just turn my feelings off and on as if I had a switch for them." We cannot just invite our feelings to come and go as we like, especially angry feelings, which are so unpredictable. But all sane human beings are capable of getting feelings under control, even strong anger. God gives us free will to make choices, and this includes choices regarding our anger. People who announce that they can't control their anger usually are signaling that they *will* not control their anger. When anger is allowed to reign supreme, we are choosing to be untamed and rebellious. To be a slave to our anger is to refuse to accept the accountability and responsibility that accompanies free will. If your tendency is to hang onto anger for an extended period of time, the thought of controlling anger seems unlikely and unnatural. Hanging onto anger runs risks, risks of losing relationships, of having accidents from seething over revenge, of maiming self or others, and of exploding hostility where you cease to be a human and become an animal.

None of this is "the abundant life" Jesus promised.

Assertiveness

When someone challenges your authority in front of others, how can you handle it in a way that actually enhances your image? When someone takes liberties or interferes with your work, how can you set limits gently and effectively? When you are pressured to promise more than you can deliver, how can you say no in a way others will respect?

When you need cooperation from people who are reluctant to give it, how can you motivate them to help willingly? When you have a great idea how can you learn to speak up confidently— and have persons listen?

The characteristics of an assertive person are very different from those of a nonassertive person. As assertive person acts in a way that shows she respects herself, is aware that she cannot always win, and accepts her limitations. She strives to make a good effort. She maintains her self-respect. An assertive person feels free to reveal himself to other persons. Basically, he says, "This is me. This is what I am, what I feel, what I think, and what I want." You do not have to guess where such persons are coming from. They can communicate with people on all levels. Communication is open, direct, honest, and appropriate. The assertive person has an active orientation to life. She knows what she wants, then goes after it with gusto.

Unfortunately, the non-assertive person confuses being liked with being respected. Nonassertive persons are conditioned to fear of being disliked or, even worse, being rejected. They are unable to recognize the difference between being selfish in a nonproductive way, and learning to "love your neighbor as yourself." Nonassertives frequently allow others to maneuver them into situations where they do not want to be. Often they are easily "hurt" by what others say, and make a point of telling others of their hurt. Since they feel inferior, their actions often mimic inferiority. Sadly, they do not use their full God-given potential.

Assertive persons should not be confused with aggressive persons, who often attack. Aggressives may be antagonistic, rude, and unpleasant to coworkers, vendors, fellow church workers, or customers. They may also be passive-aggressive, always having an excuse for what they have not completed, even though they promised to have it finished, or showing up late or not at all for a task they agreed to do. Some aggressives are whiners who complain no matter what they are asked to do. Some are thumb-twiddlers who lack motivation and initiative. Aggressives may challenge you in front of other workers or committee members. Others have negative attitudes that bring everybody down. The worrywarts often have personal problems that infringe on the workday. Some are clock-watchers, or have been around the job or the church awhile, and you wonder if they are practicing on-the-job retirement.

When you are trying to get aggressive people to work with assertive people, you need some skills. What to say and what not to say becomes of primary importance. Communication breakdowns happen frequently, and this escalates problems. Emotionally charged statements must be avoided at all costs. They always trigger a negative response, which is the antithesis of communication. I cannot overstate the importance of using clear, specific, and direct language. Actions taken need to be corrective rather than punitive. The idea in any meeting, dialogue, or conversation is to get cooperation and results without incurring resentment or damaging relationships. The bull-in-the-china-shop plan of operation leaves shambles, debris, and a lose-lose situation with no winners. Did you hear about the person who received a new boomerang and then spent the rest of his life trying to throw the old one away? The constantly returning boomerang speaks of a familiar pattern where a one-plan-person continually returns to tout his own idea, intruding on the committee process. Deal with the issue of the person's idea once and for all. If we fail to deal with unhealthy behavior, we replay patterns of dependency or self-centeredness.

To be assertive rather than aggressive means we must get ourselves moving in the right direction. We must learn to say no and make it stick without offending the other person and without feeling guilty. Learning to use our "body language" can add impact to our message. Learning specific techniques for dealing with put-downs, insults, insinuations, and unreasonable requests is vital. Often you can deflect these negative responses by asking what is meant by them, which puts the ball back in the other person's court. Simply asking the person, "Why do you ask?" changes the thrust of the question.

Always have your ideas written clearly, as well as your agenda. Learn to identify the hidden ways people may be manipulating you. Minimize defensiveness from others by using "I" language as much as you can. Learn to ask, "How would you handle this situation?" Do not hint or threaten, which only confuses the issues. Communicate as well as you can, knowing that there are some unreasonable and difficult people, but express your beliefs without fear.

Truth-Telling

Many people have difficulty having anything positive to say about anger. For many it is hard to think of any kind of positive words concerning anger. Truth-telling is a part of shepherding those who are new in the faith. As John 8:32 says, "you will know the truth, and the truth will make you free."

Being assertive means speaking up, not rudely but with conviction. We tell the truth in a way that is not vengeful. Truth can be healing, nurturing, and strengthening. Not that we always welcome the openness of truth, for it may expose vulnerability and innocence.

Our failure to speak authentically is not healthy. So often we pretend everything is fine in order to protect ourselves. It may be a misguided way of trying to protect others, but more realistically is an attempt to protect a relationship. Pretending shows our deep prohibitions against a more direct and forthright assertion. Females especially have been taught this tactic. It is attached to other prohibitions such as: "Ladies do not show anger," "Ladies must switch the subject if a discussion becomes heated," or "Always be a peacemaker, for no one likes a contentious female." Truth-telling often becomes a necessary challenge in women's lives. Harriet Lerner uses this phrase in her book *The Dance of Deception: Pretending and Truth-Telling in Women's Lives,* writing that the term seems more encompassing, courageous, and richly textured in meaning than the word *honesty.*[2]

Lerner reminds us of a tendency to organize in dichotomous categories, when in truth people are far more complex and multifaceted. She pushes us to see that truth-telling is linked to what is most essential in our lives, for it is the foundation of authenticity, intimacy, self-esteem, and integrity. "We know that closeness requires honesty, that lying erodes trust, that the cruelest lies are often 'told' by silence,"[3] but in the name of truth we hurt others, escalate anxiety, and disregard the different reality of others. She talks of her early years at Menninger Clinic, where as the sole identified feminist, she confronted and worked to raise the consciousness of her colleagues. In her zeal, she was locked in a role that made it impossible for others to hear what she said. Those of us who have had the identified role of speaking out concerning the stereotypical roles of women can easily identify with this issue.

Our gender differences are a reality, and taking that into account is not always the norm in our culture. Females are more relational, which comes partly from the way in which we are socialized. The play of girl children generally is consensual and cooperative, while the play of boy children usually is competitive

---

[2] Harriet Lerner, *The Dance of Deception: Pretending and Truth-Telling in Women's Lives* (New York: HarperCollins, 1993).
[3] Ibid., 26–27.

and team-oriented. Girl babies bond with their primary caregiver, most often a female, and that bonding holds as they grow, develop, and form new relationships. Boy babies also bond with their primary caregiver, again most often a female, but within a relatively short time they must set aside some of that relationship. For instance, boys must go into the men's room by themselves, not with the female caregiver. Little events set a pattern. Anger is experienced, but often is not allowed to be expressed. Females tend to be more verbal, especially when they are talking about feelings. Males are not exposed to talking readily about their feelings. In close interpersonal relationships men frequently feel anger as if they are playing without knowing the rules of the game.

Truth-telling becomes a problem when anger and resentment color interactions. It is not that all men are alike, of course, any more than all women are alike, plus we have the additional difficulty in perceiving accurately and processing any information shared. Our own ideas about lying and truth-telling are colored by race, class, culture, and personal history. How did your family of origin react when you told a lie? Was it all right to lie, if no one found out you were lying? Were lies a normal and accepted way of life? Who in your family vented and ranted and raved when a lie was disclosed? Was the most severe punishment reserved for those who lied? What is and what is not the truth? Is truth always absolute? Was truth discussed philosophically in your family? Do you and your spouse differ in how you perceive the truth? What about white lies; are they allowed?

Deception is seen by some as an art. If no one asks then you do not tell. For some persons, withholding information is not counted as the opposite of truth; yet it wrecks havoc with trust and depletes the level of comfort within the relationship. Politicians today are pushing family values as a simple matter, which usually means you must accept their family values as truth. Yet if we are honest, we must know that differing cultures accept differing norms. Seeing truth-telling differently is not surprising. At times we speak as if we were fully living what we are saying. One of my early supervisors when I was I training quoted regularly, "Words are more often used to conceal than to reveal."

In a couple who came to me for marital counseling, the husband was so used to relaying events to cast himself in a positive light that it created almost constant conflict. Added to this was that his wife had an old script from her extended family that proclaimed that a lie was unforgivable. It took an extended time for this pair to take into account their different heritages, and to agree on what was acceptable as truth-telling for their marriage. Nobody completely lives up to his or her own ideals and visions. Hopefully we may gradually grow into the truth we speak. Our lives always speak louder than our words, which gives us all cause for humility.

Using Good Timing

Often people comment that timing is everything, and that is certainly true with regard to anger. Remembering the fear component of anger, think of a time when your child was late and you ran a dozen scenarios (all of them negative) through your anxious mind. Then that child came in unharmed, chattering about her game or trip, and you were grateful, of course, but you also found yourself making angry remarks. Such contrasting emotions—gratitude and rage side by side. Yet when we remember that anger is often the first response to fear, it isn't really surprising. As an adolescent, our son had little concept of time, and to some extent that is still true today. I remember a time when he had permission to go to a nearby golf course, with a reminder of the time he was to be home for dinner. That time came and went, but he did not arrive. We were concerned and angry, as his behavior was causing schedule problems for four people. When he finally came home he said with great enthusiasm, "Hi folks, what's up?" Before I could speak, my husband put a hand on my arm and suggested, "Why don't we wait and talk about this tomorrow, and Jim can think about what he needs to do to make amends."

The timing for a confrontation was not good, and most assuredly hurtful words would have been said. My fear would have made my voice high and I probably would have said much too much. Jim would have been defensive because, to him, golf had been more important than suppertime. We set a time to talk the next day. Jim opened that discussion saying, "I've thought and thought and I don't know how I should be punished. Just go ahead and punish me. Trying to think of something myself is just too hard." No one won that day, but no one lost either, and we all learned the importance of making an appointment so we might have time to deal with the issue, not just our fear and anger. It is interesting to note the difference in perception as our son talked of punishment, and his father talked of making amends. We each hear in our own way, and not always accurately. Our son, in his own mind, felt he should be punished, while his dad wanted him to look at the consequences of his behavior.

George Bach, in his book *Intimate Enemy,* suggests setting an appointment to fight.[4] (Bach calls any disagreement or argument a fight.) Often it is simply not a good time to discuss a difference of opinion. An argument as one is leaving for work, or before one has a speech or presentation to make, or when one has had an especially difficult day, can be unfair at best. Setting a time to talk about it later is fair to both persons. This appointment must be kept, or it loses it effectiveness, and may become a ploy to avoid the necessary discussion.

Dealing with Anger in the Workplace

Unfortunately, the workplace is seeing an increasingly familiar phenomenon of pushing, yelling, screaming, and verbal abuse among coworkers or between managers and employees. The old Depression-era mentality in which workers were so afraid of losing their jobs they accepted without question any decree the boss pronounced, is no longer prevalent. Popes, judges, and high school principals can still make pronouncements, but few others would dare. Even if others tried, no one would pay attention. Most people are extremely uncomfortable when they are spectators to overtly expressed conflict. Loud confrontations are inappropriate expressions of anger and disrupt the work environment. They create tension and loss of productivity, and can cause such an intimidating environment that there may be legal issues.

---

[4]George Bach, *Intimate Enemy: How to Fight Fair in Love and Marriage* (New York: Morrow, 1969).

Training programs, written policies, union representatives, or open forums, by themselves will not do the job. Euphemisms that call employees "associates," "focus teams," or "critical path groups" will not keep angry feelings out of offices, plants, hospitals, or other workplaces. Employees may feel unsafe and threatened when witnessing angry incidents. Unresolved anger may contribute to employee health problems and increased absenteeism. This is, of course, an enormous cost to the organization. Anger is an emotional response to a grievance; the source of the grievance may be a person or object, or it may be rooted in cumulative stress or frustration that is acted out and expressed indiscriminately or inappropriately. Some workers have free-floating anger, and we never know where it might surface. Anger may have racial, sexual, or class components, or be tied up with some other real or imagined issue.

Expressions of anger are a learned response, and workplaces can do something about how anger is expressed on their premises. Written policies can make it clear that inappropriate expressions of anger will not be tolerated, with the penalties explicitly named. Training programs can be used to teach and encourage acceptable ways to express grievances. Policies must make clear that intimidation, threats of any kind, or unprofessional, rude expressions of anger absolutely will not be tolerated. In addition all threats will be taken seriously, even if made in a joking manner. Policies must be specific and enforced with both managers and other employees. Training in communication is needed so all can learn how to get their point across without threats or violence. Learning to recognize warning signs of violence and ways to defuse a violent situation is mandatory.

Managers and employees need training to recognize the warning signs of violence, and learn ways to defuse the situation when a coworker turns explosive or appears to be heading in that direction. Supervisors must be trained not to look away from angry incidents. Negating the importance or laughing inappropriately can escalate a situation to into violence. It is important to immediately document such a happening and discipline any inappropriate expressions of anger. Anger management skills should focus on disengagement and validation. All employees need to develop their own coping skills for dealing with day-to-day conflict, stress, irritability, and ordinary frustration of the working world.

When we feel anger at work, we need to stop and determine the source of our anger. Does our administrative superior remind us of an earlier authority figure? If your boss, by looks, actions, or gestures reminds you of a band director, a coach, or a parental figure from your past, it is time to take a long look back and see if you can resolve the old angers, humiliation, or the pain of never measuring up. Unless you resolve old issues, it will be impossible to work out a relationship with your present supervisor. When the old events happened, you were most likely not in any position to question or disagree. It may be necessary to remind yourself you are an adult now, and you can take calm, constructive action. Check to see if there is anything you can do to remedy the situation. Try the following:

- Be assertive, not aggressive.
- Ask for what you need. No one will do it for you. (Do not demand.)
- Do not get distracted. (Refocus your thoughts if needed.)
- Stick to one topic only. Do not bring up global complaints.
- Be a good listener. (Don't be thinking of a comeback.)
- Agree to think about the response you receive.
- Set another time to talk together.

If you feel anger or resentment dominates your life, seek help from a trained counselor, or see if your workplace has an employee assistance program where you can receive help. If you have been sitting on your anger all your life, only to have it build up and explode, now is the time to take a good look to see if it has turned into bitterness or hostility. Remember your own expression of anger or rage is a learned response, and if it was learned it can be unlearned. Then anger can become an emotion that is part of a whole repertoire of feelings. You are in charge of how you express your feelings. No longer are you acted upon willy-nilly, but with your own free will you have a choice of a number of behaviors to work through your anger. Once the old angers are brought to consciousness, you will be amazed how much your anger has dissipated.

Forgiveness and Anger

How difficult it is to forgive. It is especially difficult to forgive oneself. Far too many of us remember the slights, the put-downs, the imagined wrongs, and certainly those times when we were wronged. When we add anger to the equation it becomes very hard to forgive. We are aware that we live in an imperfect world, and there are no perfect solutions. Yet somehow we still feel that we should be forgiven our wrongs while we put off forgiving the wrongs of others. The psalmist in Psalm 130 gives us hope that with the Lord there is forgiveness, unfailing love and redemption. In the shame of our own broken relationships, we need to hear this word of grace. Christ forgave our sins. He gave himself up for us. He lovingly offers to replace our guilt with love, our anger with peace, and our blame with his forgiveness and love.

How much we need this soothing grace to heal the wounds from others, and it is imperative for us to heal the self-inflicted wounds, we try to bury, ignore, or forget. In Frederick Buechner's daily meditations, he writes,

> When somebody you've wronged forgives you, you're spared the dull and self-diminishing throb of a guilty conscience. When you forgive somebody who has wronged you, you're spared the dismal corrosion of bitterness and wounded pride. For both parties, forgiveness means the freedom again to be at peace inside their own skins and to be glad in each other's presence.[5]

Sometimes we hear the cry, "I can forgive, but I'll never forget!" We fool ourselves or play games with ourselves if we think we can piously say we forgive someone, but refuse to forget. Are we trying to fool God? Surely we are not. We ordinary persons must work at forgiveness. This is a process that takes time, effort, and energy. I read a newspaper story where a person had been misdiagnosed and was consumed with inoperative cancer. She had just learned death was imminent. When

---
[5]Frederick Buechner, *Wishful Thinking: A Theological ABC* (San Francisco: HarperSanFrancisco, 1993), 29.

interviewed, she said she had forgiven all who were to blame. I read on to see how long she had known of this grave error, and the paper reported she had just learned her life was almost over. Perhaps, a death sentence moves the process along, but I doubt if many of us would be so quick to achieve the process of forgiving. I suspect her husband and children will take longer to achieve their own gift of forgiving.

Serious wounds need serious healing. When we have accepted the good news in faith, we can begin to make allowances and find strength to act in love toward those who have broken relationships. We find this almost impossible to do on our own. With God's help we can be kind and compassionate to one another, forgiving each other, just as in Christ God forgave us (Eph. 4:32). Instantaneous forgiveness may be only lip service and not from the heart. Emotional wounds, whether intentional or unintentional, need to be acknowledged and given attention. Healing can come by talking with a friend who will listen patiently and sit with you in your pain. We can never find real healing as long as we continually examine and re-examine old hurts. Nor can healing take place if we dwell on blaming those who hurt us. Forgiving those who have dealt an injury to us, and letting go of past hurts, sets us free for healing and moving forward with our life.

Asking to be forgiven implies a state of being sorry, a recognition of harm, and a sincere desire to repair the rift in the relationship. It is implicit when we really want to be forgiven, to seek to make amends, to do more than to say, "I am sorry," although that is a good place to begin. Sometimes money needs to be repaid, or property must be replaced. Other times we need to seek restitution by confessing to more than one person, and while we can never take back words once they are spoken, we need to repair what damage we can. When we are sincerely sorry, and wish for forgiveness with every fiber of our being, we vow to never repeat the onerous action that brought us to this place.

6

Answers to Frequently Asked Questions about Anger

There is still more ground that warrants covering. What follows in this chapter are my responses to eight questions that often are raised concerning the gift of anger.

What If It Is Not My Anger?

It seems it is always easier to see other people's anger than our own. Pointing a finger, however, always leaves us pointing three fingers back at ourselves. We need to look within; if it is our anger, we need to accept that fact and make a decision about what to do with it. If it is not our anger, and sometimes it is not, then we have another decision to make. If someone else has a "mad in her pocket" affecting us, we need to act. We could choose to become a sort of "punching bag" for someone else's anger, but that is really no solution. We could become loud and accusatory, but again this is unpleasant and the issue remains. We could try to ignore the anger, but frequently the anger accelerates into rage. Crying and withdrawing, feeling sorry for oneself, overeating or abusing substances could be the next course of action, but that just creates at least one other problem besides the anger toward this person.

So what can I do? Is there anything that can help me live or work with this person whose anger is affecting me?

Accommodation is a frequent response to avoid destructive fighting, but this usually means someone has suppressed pain and kept silent. Often we internalize our pain, thwart our human potential, and settle for less. Thus pain roams around inside of us instead of being out in the open, where we have room to deal with it. Each of us has the capacity to sabotage ourselves internally, resulting in indigestion, headaches, high blood pressure, colon disorders, and other illnesses that can be caused by anger and stress. Or we may redirect our anger and frustrations by attacking and being unpleasant to other people who are not at fault. We can become less loving by shutting down and showing neither positive nor negative emotion. We may refuse to allow ourselves to feel any emotion.

Instead of expressing appropriately their needs, many resort to manipulation of the anger-filled person who is the source of their pain, using tricks, ploys, and devices to try to change the other person's behavior. Such tactics may make those who use them feel guilty for having their own needs, and to condemn themselves for being demanding and critical. Finally, they find subtle ways of hurting their spouse, boss, or coworker by allowing the "other" to get into trouble they could have prevented. They may shun, ignore, or go around the person, while passively-aggressively following orders to the letter, knowing it is not what the other wants. They complain to others, but never confront the behavior directly. This kind of passive-aggressive behavior is not productive, and has been compared to slamming a swinging door—you may swing very hard, but you don't get any bang for your buck. The other person may be confused and have not the slightest idea of what you want or need. Communication comes to a standstill, and the breach in the relationship widens.

Accommodating becomes an unhealthy process because it stifles and submerges negative feelings—sometimes for years. I had a client who lived with an alcoholic spouse. She was miserable. She had accommodated his alcoholic binges, lied to his boss by saying he was ill when he was hung over, made excuses for him to his children and his mother, and never disagreed with him no matter how obnoxious he became. She was referred to me by her doctor because of gastrointestinal problems that did not respond to treatment. She was quick to tell me that her religion would not allow her to divorce her husband, so she supposed there was nothing I could do to help her. To her surprise, I agreed with her. There was nothing I could do to bring about first-order change in her life, but there were a number of things she could do. I asked if she was willing and got her to commit. First I told her I respected her religious position and I wanted her to take it even further. She immediately asked, "How do I do that? I will do anything." I said, "Never lie for him again. If he wants his boss called, he will have to tell his own lies." She protested, "But what about his job?" I shrugged, asking her how she thought God felt about all those lies she had told over the years. With new resolve, she left my office saying, "I'll do it. I really will do it."

When she came in again she said, "I did it. It was the hardest thing I ever had to do, but I did it. He could not believe I wasn't going to call his boss." I inquired as to what followed, and with a smile she said, "He drank a pot of black coffee, took a cold shower, and went grumbling off to work. I thanked God over and over." She continued to come to therapy, but had more trouble not making excuses for her husband to the children. She had seen herself as the emotional manager of the family and had always explained why their dad could not be at ballgames, class plays, or recitals. It was hard to give up that powerful role. My unseen ally was her son, who one day told her in disgust, "Aw, come on, Mom, you know Dad doesn't come because nothing is as important to him as alcohol." She was stunned, but she finally accepted the truth and suggested the children ask their dad for what they needed from him. It turned out that Dad made a much better response to his children than he had to the filtered request from his wife. She did the same with his mother's requests for coming over for a meal, forcing the husband to communicate with his mother directly. Hardest of all was giving up her tricks, ploys, and manipulation in dealing with her husband, but this paid the biggest dividend of all. Over a course of two years he drank less and less, eventually going to AA, where he was assigned a sponsor who had been in the depths of alcoholism himself and was not fooled by any of the husband's frequent excuses. My client reported at a final session that she was closer to God than ever before in her life, as well as to her husband and children, and as a bonus her gastrointestinal problems were much better.

Each of us has some kind of power over the persons we are in relationship with, even when we perceive ourselves to be the weakest party. In one way or another we tend to use our power. Sometimes we use power by withholding. It may be sex, money, privileges, relationships with family, respect, or good service. We may order, threaten, or give warnings. Some appeal to a higher authority by complaining to the boss, calling the parent of the one to whom you are married, or a really low blow, threatening to quit praying for the person. One client reported she told her husband, after yet another episode of binge drinking, "You can just go to hell, for all I care." We may say they do not deserve our services or our love, but if we are withholding that which we have contracted to supply, who has broken the contract? Power plays often bring on more conflict, but it is common among those who cannot, or will not, fight. If you have used your best efforts to heal a relationship, have examined your own anger, and find you are still reacting with pain, you may have to accept that life is too short to live this way. You may need to make a serious change. Quit your job. Move away. Leave. Seek help.

What If I Like My Anger?

Why would anyone like his or her anger? I asked this question in a seminar I was leading. In this group of bright, articulate persons, I was surprised to have a number of them quickly respond. One held a position of authority with a newspaper and believed his anger was an asset in keeping his personnel "on their toes." A father of four said he maintained his anger in order to be in control and not to be questioned about everything he said. One woman said, "I've kept my anger because it is all I have left from my marriage."

It was interesting that many males spoke, but only one female. Later in the week I received a note from a woman who had attended the seminar. She wrote that she hesitated to speak out because of the personal nature of why she kept her anger. She wrote a poignant letter about being sexually abused by an uncle when she was a young girl. It was a letter filled with pain, which touched me so much I called her and asked her to come in and talk with me. She had attempted one time to get help, and felt emotionally raped by the person from whom she sought help. Unfortunately, the person she had seen was not a competent therapist, or even a compassionate person. In no uncertain terms she told me she elected to hold on to her anger to remind her she could not trust anyone. I thanked her for being honest with me, and she left my office.

More than a year later she called and asked if I would see her therapeutically. When I agreed, she came ready to work on her rage. I asked her, "Why now?" After all this time and a vile experience, why had she decided to come now? It was months before she was comfortable enough to tell her story in bits and pieces. The incompetent person she had seen had told her there was only one way to work through her abuse, and that was to confront the abuser and file charges against him, and she believed him. Because of the power and reputation of her abuser, she felt this was impossible and that she would be scarred and blemished for life if she went public. She worked at venting her rage through gestalt, journaling, talking to an empty chair, and with therapeutic imaging. She also planned some events to give pleasure to herself, which she had never allowed before because she felt flawed and dirty, even though it was not her fault she was abused. But none of it had worked. How difficult it is for an abused child not to feel guilty, when a trusted adult repeatedly tells her she is at fault. At the last session I had with this woman she told me, "I no longer like my anger, nor do I need to keep it any longer, but I do like myself now!"

Learning to use our anger effectively requires some letting go. It is not our responsibility to fix or change other people. We can't tell others how to think, feel, or behave, even if we would like to. Nor do we have to passively accept or go along with any behavior. To decide to live and let live can be a denial of self if this means not clarifying what is acceptable and desirable in a relationship, and what is not. If we are chronically angry or bitter in important relationships, it is a signal that too much of the self has been compromised. We may need to speak with greater clarity. Being vague can become a habit, so you can "waffle" and not be responsible. To be in a healthy relationship, honesty, clear communication, and careful listening are mandatory. If you are not sure about your position or where you come down on a particular issue, then say so. Gather more information, read, talk with those of varying opinions and make up your own mind. It is not wrong to take the needed time to decide what you think and feel.

Psychological protection accounts for many people keeping, and even surrounding themselves with, anger. Because they have been hurt when they were young, naive, or vulnerable, they assume they must constantly protect themselves or become a victim once again. Understandably they have no desire to be a victim, but by becoming assertive they can claim their own power without remaining constantly angry. Such anger makes relationships difficult at best, and often breaks the relationship altogether. These individuals are perceived by others to be cantankerous, aggressive, mean, and hard to get along with. In business, it is easier to shop elsewhere or contract with a new company. In relationships with family and friends we must work at it.

What Triggers My Anger?

It is not unusual to do Monday-morning quarterbacking concerning our anger. I often hear clients say, "I didn't even know I was angry until later," or "Open mouth, insert foot. Now I have to live with the consequences of my anger." Anger arousal is identifiable, with some effort on our part. If we can learn what triggers our anger, we are on the way to dealing with anger, and using it as an important tool in our interpersonal relations.

Each of us has a self-image that shapes our personality and emerges in our interaction with others. Some of what we have been taught as the "right way" to behave seems to be nonnegotiable, and often this is the source of conflict with those closest to us. Little things that we were not consciously taught can become guiding principles. When a man and a woman marry they bring "baggage" from their families—of origin. In his family, they always opened their Christmas gifts on Christmas Eve. In hers, they always opened gifts Christmas morning. Other variations enter into the discussion. Each believes his or her way is the only way and to change would be disloyal to family.

Personality characteristics ignored in courtship loom large. While they were dating, when he became demanding in order to get a table at a restaurant, she thought he was forceful; now she sees him as a bully. Before marriage, when she withdrew and became very quiet, he considered her thoughtful; now he sees her as sullen and noncommunicative. Who changed? Neither. We tend to see and even hear what we want to see and hear during courtship.

While we may become angry with our family of origin, we are very protective if others find fault with our family. Even to think of celebrating Christmas on a different day may imply criticism of our family. Then there is the tremendous sentimentality surrounding Christmas itself. Some of that sentimentality can grow into rigidity, and woe to anyone who would dare change any part of Christmas. Then schedules become overcrowded with decorating, gift buying and wrapping, entertaining, and being entertained. Fatigue is another important factor in anger arousal. Others add they have felt attacked when asked to change *meaningful* rituals. With anger arousal at a high peak it is simple for anger to reach a crescendo with words flying irresponsibly. The old television commercial comes to mind: A person has seriously eaten too much, and looking very miserable groans, "I can't believe I ate the whole thing!" Even so, anger grows if small disagreements are not talked about and resolved. And emotionally, we can't believe we have swallowed so much anger. It is easy to laugh at such anger in relationships, as long as they are not our own relationships. Common topics of marital quarrels are vacations, in-laws, money, sex, children, and use of leisure time. There are some ways of resolving or reducing conflict without compromising your basic stance:

- Separate nonnegotiable from unmentionable. Discuss what you see as your core position. Explain your feelings and your boundaries.
- Separate "can't" from "won't." Discuss whether changing would threaten who you feel you are.
- Don't shut the door. How you have felt and how you are feeling now are not inevitable predictors of how you will feel in the future.

- Weigh your own needs against the needs of your partner.
- Attempt to think outside the lines. This fresh look may give you options.
- For now, put the discussion on the shelf, making an appointment to talk later.
- Meditate and pray. This often gives a fresh perspective.

Anger arousal may be psychological protection to hide our feelings. If in your family of origin tears were not tolerated, anger may be a way of not feeling tender feelings. Some of us cry when listening to a lovely piece of music or seeing a beautiful sunset, but this behavior may be foreign or even bizarre if you have been reared to think it is a sign of weakness. With anger there is a comfort zone where you may be loud, competitive, and seemingly unfeeling. This, of course, is not true, but the illusion remains. This behavior is more often male, but not exclusively, as females may have also been socialized to think tender feelings are a sign of weakness. The injunction, "Don't cry!" is still heard in too many families, grocery stores, malls, and even in hospitals where "being brave" is valued more than honesty.

Being dependent can raise anger to a boiling point. If you visit any rehabilitation facility, the anger level is noticeable, and small wonder as patients must slowly, painstakingly learn to do ordinary tasks they have taken for granted for years and years. Walking, climbing stairs, buttoning a shirt, peeling potatoes, drinking from a straw, putting on make-up, shaving, and a other tasks are now goals to be achieved with a maximum effort. Anger is often a motivating force for a patient to "show" the world he is not dependent. Since anger is an action force, this can be healthy— as opposed to depression, which is withdrawal from others and feelings pulled inward, which can lead to suicidal thoughts. Physical therapists welcome anger over depression any day. It is difficult for family members to witness, but the rage may be a declaration of refusal to accept the unacceptable.

I recall seeing a patient in a rehab center who had tried to take his own life. After seeing him briefly several times, I needed him to sign some papers relative to insurance payments. He started to write his name and when it did not go well he threw the pen across the room and clear out into the hall. An orderly came into the room and very calmly sat down in a chair next to me. The patient cursed and threw his pillow, followed by his empty urinal and a water pitcher. Still calm, the orderly helped the patient to a sitting position and asked him if he was ready to begin work. They left the room, and I gathered up my papers knowing I would return another day. This nice, quiet man began to make progress with his physical therapy. It was a long, arduous process, and while he frequently became discouraged, his anger kept him going. If we are honest, we can relate to the rage he felt at being incapacitated and dependent.

How Can I Live with Frustration?

In interpersonal relationships it is vital for us to know when to quit pressing an issue. We do not have to have the last word in every disagreement. Nor do we have to squeeze out every last drop of rage when we are expressing our anger. Who made us the umpire of "rightness" or the "den mother" of never ever being wrong? Minor irritations are just that—minor. Every time we do not see eye to eye does not need to become a major confrontation. If we feel we must win every time we disagree, we are setting up the next argument. It is important to express how we feel and then leave a way open to resolve future conflicts. What an accomplishment! With some issues it is more important for the other person to save face than for us to declare a victory. If he is an expert on football, and she is a casual onlooker, does putting him down give the hoped-for satisfaction?

Who among us has not had an evening tarnished by the bickering of the couple at the dinner party who delighted in putting each other down? Such irascible folks may find their invitations diminishing in proportion to their ubiquitous disagreements. We must learn to forgive. Persons do not live up to our expectations. Our expectations are just that—ours. Important people in our lives can fail to be what we need them to be. If we are honest, we have all failed someone at one time or another. I am not advocating you become a victim, but if you dwell on your victimhood, you are then victimized in a new way. Some angers must be let go, so we can forgive others and ourselves. To ruminate on our anger accomplishes nothing.

If you are constantly frustrated with your anger or someone else's anger, it is time to make some changes. Recurring anger signals a problem that is not being dealt with effectively. If you live with shouting matches or a "cold war" of banked hostility, it is time to take an honest look at the source of the problems and how they can be solved. Make an appointment now to work through your issues, which are not going to go away with wishful thinking. Call a counselor and make an appointment to talk about your recurring anger or the "armed camp" that is your home base. Evaluate how comfortable that counselor is in talking about your anger and whether or not you are comfortable with her or him. If the counselor is not comfortable with anger, in all probability you will not receive the help you need. You want a counselor who will help you gain insight into your anger and help you craft solutions.

Webster's New World Dictionary defines frustrate: "1. to cause to have no effect; bring to nothing; counteract; nullify 2. to prevent from achieving an objective; foil; baffle; defeat 3. to prevent from gratifying certain impulses or desires, either conscious or unconscious." Frequently clients tell me they are not angry, they are frustrated. If you read this definition carefully you will note frustration seems to be about what the other person does to you. There is no claiming of our own feelings, rather a complaint concerning what others do to us. Frustration frequently involves "you messages:" "You baffle me." "You counteract my wishes." "You prevent me from reaching my objective." Change such messages to "I" messages. "I am baffled when it seems you are not listening to me." "I must not be making myself clear when you counteract my wishes." "I need your help in reaching my objective." Such communication opens the way for dialogue, rather than blame that may cause defensiveness.

When we angrily confront another person, convinced that truth is on our side, we often move the situation from bad to worse. When anxiety is at a peak, we divide into opposing camps and lose our capacity to see all sides of an issue. The capacity for creative problem solving is diminished or lost. As the emotional climate heats up, we have to struggle harder to uncover our own truth, to hear each other, or to not leave the room. When this happens, frustration is rampant. Communication ceases. The "FUD Factor" (fear, uncertainty, and doubt) urges us to lash out, withdraw, burst into tears, or act self-righteous. Anger wears many disguises, many of which are experienced as sorrow, depression, addiction, or workaholic activity. The many faces of anger can eat away at our souls and prevent us from reaching our objective—and we experience frustration of the first order. Frustration tells us about damaged relationships and losses not grieved, but it also open up a pathway for change and newness. Hope is not always born of sunshine. Frustration worked out can be the cradle of hope and the birth of faith.

How Do I Avoid the Blame Game?

It is tempting to view all relationships in terms of cause and effect. If I am angry, someone caused me to be angry. If another person with whom I am in a relationship is angry, then I must be to blame. What did I do to cause this anger? Or we may make a judgment that the other person has no right to feel anger. Family members, couples, work groups, or other important small groups in our life often take responsibility for others' feelings and reactions. They may blame the ones they are in close relationship with for their own thoughts, emotions, and behavior.

We are each responsible for our own behavior. We are not responsible for any other person's behavior or reactions, nor are they responsible for ours. This may well fly in the face of what you learned as a child. You may have memories of being told, "Now look what you have done. Your behavior sent your mother to bed with a headache." Or "Why do you make your brother so angry? Since you are the oldest, you should know better than that." Such old tapes still play in our heads, causing us to feel either guilt for causing others to suffer, or blame for what others have caused to happen to us. It is vital we learn how to be free from either guilt or blame.

We need to learn to share our reactions without holding the other person hostage for causing our feelings, or blaming ourselves for others' reactions to our choices or actions. We cannot hand over our responsibility to others. I once had an administrator who talked one way and acted in another way. It was confusing at best, and led to frequent misunderstandings among the staff. My own confusion was compounded because I spent the first six months on the job believing what he said. He talked at length about honesty, but at times he was what he called "political." My colleagues seemed to accept that for him, "political" was less than honest. My expectations for this person were that he would be congruent. He was not. It took time for me to recognize that my expectations were just that—my expectations. They were valid expectations, but they were mine, thus I was responsible for them, not my administrator. The responsibility for his actions rested with him.

As we think about our own workplaces, we are aware of little vignettes we see and hear every day. As previously mentioned, a worker may make a trip to the restroom with a rigid back and fast steps after a confrontation with the boss, but staunchly declare that nothing is wrong. { When one person is the brunt of anger from the supervisor, all the other workers try to busy themselves or look elsewhere, but are careful not to miss a word. Then they divide into two distinct camps—those for the boss and those for the poor worker, who could have been them. Blame is assigned. They may not be clear about what the issues are, but they make assumptions and place blame on someone, feeling glad it is not they on the hot seat.

Holiday time brings out anger in the extended family. Every Christmas I have one or more clients who declare they cannot go home at Christmas because their sister or brother or some other relative will be there. When you try to get a picture of what has happened, it is often a confused jumble of images. Someone has done to them what they consider a wrong. They are waiting for an apology and will not go until they receive one. I asked a male client in this situation what he needed to hear from his brother before he could return to the family gathering. He became ill at ease, then left the session early. I told him I wanted him to write, before his next appointment, what he needed to hear from his brother. The next week he was embarrassed as he confessed he could not remember exactly what his brother had said or done. I suggested that his brother in all probability could not recall either. So he called his brother and they met, reluctantly, for coffee. Neither recalled what had happened, but each blamed the other. My client began to laugh and his brother joined him. Both of them went home for Christmas at the same time that year.

What Do I Do about Anger in the Church?

When there is trouble in our church family it seems to hit us in the pit of our stomach. Since our place of worship is usually seen as our sanctuary when anything is wrong in our lives, it creates difficulty when we feel we have lost this place of safety. One of my friends fervently said, "Church fights are the worst fights of all." When I asked her what she meant, she responded with impatience: "You know, everybody knows you have been deeply cut, but they act as if nothing has happened." She told me how in her church a young person was asked to give up her Sunday school class, and she perceived this as unfair. When she complained, the authorities responded that it was none of her concern and refused to give her any further information. My friend felt they were being judgmental and declared her feelings were hurt, but denied she had any anger. Church secrets had closed communication and caused pain. My friend was obviously angry, but she deemed it inappropriate to be angry about a church matter. But angry feelings need to be dealt with in a way to dissipate them, without stockpiling them to create indigestion or depression.

Our God must be amused as we differentiate as to where we allow ourselves to feel anger. Feelings are not good in one place and bad in another. It is what we choose to do with our feelings that brings value judgments. If church leaders can learn to be a nonanxious presence, it can put a church school on track for growth and change. The best leaders are not reactive or blaming but are open to listening without prior judgment. A former client described a person who made judgments without facts as having a mind like concrete: all mixed up and permanently set. Anxious systems usually have anxious leaders, though leaderless systems are certainly more likely to be anxious also. If we can focus on the strength of our people, rather than the fundamental weakness inherent in being human, we can coach people to be winners. It is important to remember that systems can be flawed. When this is true, a systemic evaluation is needed so we do not scapegoat the innocent. Obviously we are not always going to agree; how dull if we did? But hopefully we can facilitate dialogue without cutting off those who disagree with us, just because we are the leadership.

I continue to be amazed at the nit-picking remarks that are made about church leadership. To say to your pastor that you do not like his or her sermon is not helpful. It is helpful to say that you would like to dialogue about a specific issue in the sermon, and ask when you can get together. To complain about what *they* do at *that* church are remarks that tear down. To ask to speak to the chair of the committee or task force about a project shows interest and a willingness to learn. Talking about church leaders in a gossipy, derogatory manner tends to belittle the speaker. To offer to help teach or lead shows a spirit of cooperation and a willingness to experience growth. Some church families are quick to adore, and just as quickly their adoration turns to scorn. They are quick to talk about their feelings without ever trying to discover whence these feelings emerged. Low self-esteem may lead to hurt feelings that the church leader is clueless about, not knowing what has gone before. If we don't recognize our own feelings, including anger, we may be too quick to deify, or to crucify!

The genesis of anger in a church setting can be difficult and seemingly impossible to trace. Spiritual stagnation is present, and the leadership is fatigued. Conversations about what is wrong with the church are held without anyone advancing workable plans. Most church members seem content to go on as if nothing is wrong, while backbiting and distancing become the norm. As a church falters, a small group must agree on a mission and then engage the congregation (or at least a larger group in the congregation) to help them set goals, discover their unique mission, set up a plan to implement ways of being in ministry in their community, and work to facilitate their own spiritual formation. The change in the ministry of such a church is dramatic. No longer do they play the blaming game. Apathy is no longer seated in every pew. Stagnation no longer solidifies the status quo. With a mission, they are serious, and they are motivated.

Anger seems to swirl through our society, and our churches are not immune. Simplistic answers abound; you hear blame placed on working women, divorce, single parents, lazy young people, the lack of a work ethic, an affluent society. The list grows as we seek an easy answer. It is always easier to assign blame than search for elusive causes. There is uncertainty about whether certain changes are good or evil, with an almost palpable sense of grief and betrayal as an old way passes, and what seemingly is more insecure emerges. The anger pervades society, and our churces are not immune, leaving them unable to minister. Perhaps like Paul we sadly lament, "The good I would, I do not."

How Do I Handle the Anger that Accompanies Grief?

How difficult it is to admit we are angry with someone who died. Someone we loved is now where we cannot tell them our anger, our despair, our feelings of helplessness, or even how much we loved them. It was so sudden, and then it was all over. Too late to utter the forgiveness not offered or the compliment we failed to give. Why did this happen? Why did this have to happen to me? So many feelings surge through us at times of grief, it is hard to sort them all out. If anger is a stranger to our emotional repertoire, we find ourselves almost choking with an emotion we cannot identify. Frequently we enter a process of rationalization, telling ourselves over and over we can't be angry, because we loved them. And we did, but living in any close, intimate relationship can create anger. Those we love have the power to create an anger within us greater than any other anger. Or to be more accurate, we give the power to those we love to create angry feelings in us, for no one can make us angry. The feelings are ours. And remember feelings just are, they are not right or wrong. The judgment comes from us, not from our emotions.

The depth of our feelings is overwhelming. Clients who have suffered a serious loss talk about wanting to hit something. But what can you hit to make the impact needed for a loss of this magnitude? Investing in an old-fashioned punching bag can be prudent and wise, and this holds true for females as well as males. Small children love to have a "permission" object to hit, and a small, anchored bag is a safe place to vent rage and anger without harming others or themselves. Anger at the death of a loved one is so unthinkable, so unspeakable; we find ourselves denying our feelings to others as well as to ourselves, with no resolution of our grief. As I wrote in my last book, *And Not One Bird Stopped Singing,* anger can take many forms: anger with the one who is gone, anger with the doctor or the hospital, anger with the person for not taking better care of himself or herself, rage at poor choices the deceased made, or anger with the church, the pastor, or with God.[1]

Our anger with God can be a white-hot fire, but we are "too nice" to give vent to our feelings, since we have a perverted notion that we need to protect God. How absurd! As if God needed protection from us. If we can be honest with our own feelings, make a careful assessment about a healthy response to our hostility, we can find release and peace. This is a time when we must acknowledge our anger and look to see what is underneath it. Early in my clinical training, I had a supervisor who said over and over, "All behavior has meaning. If you will really live your life, and not just exist, you must examine your feelings and learn what they mean." If you are angry with God because God did not save your loved one, then you must work through your anger, or it will impede your relationship with God.

To have a physical action as an available outlet can help us allow ourselves a variety of feelings, and frequently moves us from our "pity party" to a realization of the fear behind our anger. Fear precedes anger. Parents know the fear when they look away for a minute, and then discover the small child is suddenly gone. Once the child steps out from where he or she has hidden, the fearful parent quickly becomes the angry parent. This scene is replayed in shopping centers and grocery stores regularly. Death may bring to our memory an abandonment experience, and we feel those the old feelings as well as the present grief. In our unconscious the two experiences merge,

---

[1] Doris Moreland Jones, *And Not One Bird Stopped Singing: Coping with Transition and Loss in Aging* (Nashville: Upper Room Books, 1997).

and our anxiety is doubled. Knowing this does not change what has happened, but knowledge is power, and knowing opens the door to healing.

Can Therapy Help?

The link between anger and aggression is easily assumed. Contemporary therapists look at angry outbursts as the result of a series of events: perceived insults, frustrations, extreme sensitivity to threats, and stress, which are interpreted through beliefs about these insults and result in emotional and physical responses. The task of the psychotherapist is to have the person recognize his or her anger, and seek to short-circuit the anger response before it rockets out of control, by encouraging clients to question their beliefs about insults and provocation. Learning to relax the body by deep breathing, tensing and releasing muscles, and evaluating the inflammatory situation can change the emphasis. The idea is not to act out blindly, nor fly off the handle, but to look at an incident with the third eye.

What is happening that has brought me to a flare point? Am I sure this response is slanted toward me? Why am I reacting so strongly to this statement? Could I be overreacting? Was it an accident I didn't get the word about the change of time for the meeting? Come on, did they really mean to leave me out of the loop? Do I tend to become paranoid when I am stressed and physically tired? Who else in my family of origin acted this way when they felt left-out? Is this real or is this the way I have been conditioned to act? I wonder if I should take a walk and clear my head before I make any response to this event? These are the questions a good therapist helps you to think about before you act, rather than after.

Many persons have never learned how to act or react when criticized. They immediately go on the defensive and theoretically throw the first punch without checking out the situation. Those who were coddled or overly protected in childhood have an unrealistic picture of life, believing they can do no wrong. They see only two responses: to come out swinging or lie down and play dead. A relationship with a competent counselor can help you learn a response that is assertive and effective, and can teach responses of questioning, gathering new information, asking for suggestions, or even using humor effectively. Such responses do not get you fired or ostracized, and they let you move on.

There is a definite physical side to anger, and dealing with the body can help tame the mind. Deep breathing is helpful, or visualizing a calming experience gives you an opportunity to get beyond the immediate. Ask for a time-out and escape briefly with a walk or a run up and down the stairs, or seek out a cup of coffee or a cold drink—all of which gives you time to be in control and to act rather than react. Reactions are frequently physical without thought to the consequences. It is possible to learn to see your anger as a friend, and then make a decision about how you will deal with your anger. When someone is shouting at you in anger, you can diminish the energy by responding in a low, soft tone of voice. This is as effective in a controversial meeting of a task force as it is with overtired children.

We can use our anger as a guide to determine our innermost needs, values, and priorities. Truthfully we may not know about our needs, or at best we are unclear about them. A therapeutic relationship can help you prioritize your goals and help you achieve them. Many of us are chronically angry or bitter about our relationships, not knowing that too much of our self has been compromised, and are unaware of what options are open to us. We know the words, "You will know the truth, and the truth will make you free," but we have difficulty being set free without a guide or mentor. We all have old tapes, family injunctions, bad precedents, and poor examples; and to unpack that baggage we need some objectivity that is lacking as we go over and over the same terrain. I am asked sometimes if I think everyone needs therapy. I usually respond, "I certainly think everyone deserves therapy." And I do think so.

There is a form of therapy called gestalt. Gestalt is a German word meaning "whole," and gestalt psychology is a process of psychotherapy developed by Frederick (Fritz) Perls. It is a practical kind of psychotherapy. Gestalt therapists maintain that depression is due to one's perceived failure to live up to the expectations of others. This means that the depressed look to others for direction and strength rather than within themselves. Depression is distinguished from sadness. Depression is a state where we feel immobilized. Depression is often brought about by denial. Getting in touch with our feelings is a very practical thing to do in psychotherapy. It takes longer to describe than to experience. The hitting of the punching bag or a pillow is a gestalt to release the locked in and often unknown denial and anger which we hide from ourselves. A brisk walk, swimming several laps, vacuuming the carpets, chopping wood, or whipping eggs and butter for a cake all have therapeutic qualities of gestalt. One of my former clients learned to work out the stress in his life by making and giving away yeast bread. He reported that no matter how up-tight he was when he left his demanding profession, putting dough to rise and then kneading it brought a great sense of calm and peace to him. A gestalt that works for us helps us to bring to consciousness the strength within ourselves. If this is not workable for you, then ask your pastor or your physician for a referral to a counselor to facilitate your discovery of that which keeps you from being all that God created you to be.

7

Children and Anger

Angry children have erupted into the news with an alarming frequency. Most persons seem to sigh deeply, then put it out of their mind until the next incidence of violence. Many so-called experts have a plethora of reasons, excuses, theories, or a "spin" on what happened and why. Simplistic answers abound, such as too much television, working mothers, absentee dads, heavy-metal music, sugared cereal, or the church not doing its work as it should. While all of these may have a shard of truth, they are not the cause of violent, out-of-control, destructive behavior on the part of our children and young people. Why is it so much easier to blame than to seek solutions to end this scourge in our communities? I suppose it is because blaming takes no thought, energy, action, or hard work.

If we are serious about this problematic issue, we must do more than give lip service with canned answers to this complex, multicultural, and multifarious state of affairs. It is going to take the combined planning and thinking of persons who are more interested in solutions than in being one hundred percent right, who will refrain from simplistic blaming of "those" other persons. It will require a serious perusal of events and facts, as well as a study of the economic, sociological, psychological, and theological issues in our culture. Such an in-depth coalition would harvest data from a multi-lateral pool of information supplied from a variety of sources, without preconceived notions of the expected outcome. Such a study/seminar/inquiry would need the best minds possible, as well as the cooperation and input of ordinary folks from all walks of life.

We will have to look deep into our own hearts and minds at the thoughts and feelings we have about rage, anger, and violence. Do we say we believe in one thing, but actually live out our life in a different way? One of the widely used techniques by television newspeople is to interview persons on the street following a violent episode, asking them their opinion of what has happened. Much too frequently, the responses from *hoi polloi* seem to reflect a violence that is alarming. There is a vengeance that appears to infect their voice and demeanor that takes us back to the days of the Roman Empire, or to bullfights, with the spectators screaming for blood. Is this untapped, perhaps unknown cell of vengeance and violence a hidden carcinoma waiting to divide into multiple cells, divide again and again, and spread out into our world? How frightening!

My concern is that we are so used to covering our less than nice thoughts that we do not even recognize them. We carefully conceal them under a veneer of goodness, and continue to live as if anger were not a problem for us. Acting as if we were perfect claims a large portion of our time and effort, as if playing the role often enough will, in fact, make it real. We all have a dark side, even when we deny it. As Carl Jung pointed out, we all have a shadow side that we try to keep hidden, not only from others, but also from ourselves. Jung believed that our behavior is conditioned not only by our individual and racial history but also by our aims and aspirations. He believed that our shadow side may be hidden from the public by the persona, or repressed into the personal unconscious. Actually, the shadow gives vitality to personality and helps us to be well rounded, if we can acknowledge this so called dark side of ourselves.

Anger Involving Children

We are more aware of children than ever before. One of my attorney friends jokingly says this is the decade of the kids. In one sense, it is as if the media, the service organizations, the government, and even the church has just discovered children. This is not a bad thing to happen, but one does wonder where all this attention was down through the years. Of course, culturally, children are more important than they were in times past when children were to be "seen and not heard." At the grocery recently I overheard a parent consulting a two-year-old concerning his preference for chocolate or yellow birthday cake, with five customers waiting with varying degrees of impatience while the child changed his mind back and forth. The anger around the bakery counter in that supermarket was evident to all but the parent.

Divorce has had a tremendous impact on parent-child relationships. Divorce seems to bring out the most vicious kind of anger between a mother and father. Even if they will not admit anger at the former spouse for the way they perceive they were treated, they can get up a full head of steamy anger concerning the children. In the counseling office I have heard accusations against the former spouse of every offense imaginable: physical abuse, emotional abuse, sexual abuse, negligence, disinterest, spending money on themselves that was supposed to be spent on the children, and never playing with the children or participating in school events. It is rare indeed for a parent to declare an ex-spouse a fine parent.

Unfortunately, many of the offenses actually have happened. But often, when the accusations are scrutinized, they are found to be the result of anger or hostility spilling out. A lowering of self-esteem often accompanies divorce, and the "wounded" partner seeks recourse through blaming the other parent. It is vital that such anger or hostility be worked through rather than seething and allowing bitterness to corrode the already shaky relationship. The marriage may be over, but the relationship between the two parents goes on. Frequently such anger lies dormant for years, coming front and center at the weddings and graduations of the children, tainting supposedly happy occasions. Ironically, just when the focus should be on the child, the spotlight is on the parents, who never conceded they had problems with anger. Small wonder adult children think twice about including long-divorced, still-feuding parents in family celebrations.

Children often retain anger that is not really theirs. If one parent "bad-mouths" the other or uses the child as a surrogate confessor or "friend," the tendency is for the child to take sides against the other parent. The child carries a load of anger for years that is the parent's, not the child's in any conceivable way. What an unfair way to dupe an innocent child. This may also happen when the parent has never resolved issues with his or her own parents. The child hears how the grandparent has been unfair, probably through a perception that a sibling received preferential treatment, and then the grandchild takes on the parent's anger. Dealing with secondhand anger is convoluted by many layers of deceit, half-truths, and assumptions. This is another very good reason to work through our anger before we contaminate another generation.

Children may incorrectly deduce that parental anger, and even divorce, is their fault. Such guilt may preclude children of divorce from venturing into marital relationships, as the children believe they are jinxes. Children of parents going through a divorce often tell me it is their fault that their parents are no longer living together. When I ask them to tell me about that, it is not unusual for them to respond, "They were arguing, and I asked if I could go to play with my friend. They screamed at me, saying I was selfish and only thinking of myself, and I guess I was. But I didn't mean for Mommy and Daddy not to live in the same house any more." Words spoken in anger, if not decoded, may leave a small child feeling to blame for the upheaval of divorce. Parents are often so caught up in their own issues they forget the possible consequences of harsh words.

No one can be all things to all people, and this is especially true when our emotional circuits are overloaded. All children begin with the same amount of self-esteem, but how quickly it can be eroded. Simple questions or statements can douse ego strength, such as: "Why are you wearing that? Why can't you get a hundred on your spelling paper like I used to do? Your sister doesn't cause any trouble; why can't you be like her? You really do wreck havoc in my life. You couldn't sing if you had the tune in a bucket. Come and sit down; you act just like your dad, and you certainly don't want to be like him. Your mother was flighty, and you act just like her, so straighten up right now." Work to keep your anger away from children or grandchildren. Go to a counselor or to a divorce recovery group, but please do not cripple your children with issues that are not theirs. It will be a good investment for you and your children.

Violence in Our Schools

Time magazine's June 29, 1998, issue offered the following statistics: one million students in grades 6 to 12 took a gun to school during the year of the article. Sixty-three percent of students who took guns to school said they had threatened to harm another person. The decrease from 1993 to 1998 in the number of students who brought guns to school was 36 percent. I wonder if that number was supposed to encourage us?

There is a frightening shift seen in the violence in schools from single-victim shootings to multiple shootings, indiscriminate shooting of a large number of persons who had little or nothing to do with the events that led to the problem. There seem to be more firepower, more victims, and more callousness. Some of the real-life scenes of semiautomatic weapons blasting into a crowd of school children have an uncanny resemblance to cinematic catastrophes, causing us to wonder if young killers are acting out what they have seen on the big screen. Movie roles show violence as fun, and video games portray rewards for killing, sometimes hour after hour. It is a combustible mix when violence is shown as exciting and thrilling. Access to semiautomatic weapons is easy, and young people seem to be already very angry. Sometimes the lines blur between good and bad guys, making heroes out of any who fight or mix humor with violence. Copycat violence is a reality in our society. Just as we have experienced how adolescent suicide can influence others to attempt suicide; violence begets violence.

Many children have been conditioned to think of guns as that which can be used to solve problems. Children need to know that guns are lethal weapons. They are not toys to play with. Our schools must be more responsible and proactive in preventing bullying, fighting, and violence. Zero tolerance for violence is mandatory. No longer can we ignore such behavior and spout platitudes such as "boys will be boys." It is more accurate to say boys and girls will be dead or seriously injured, if violence is not stopped. Why are we continually surprised when violence erupts in seemingly safe small towns? After all, with more than two hundred million guns privately owned, it is amazing that we do not have more killings. *USA Today,* June 26–28, 1998, reported that "this is four guns for every child ages 6–16!" Also, "three out of every five TV programs contain violence, and 89 percent of all TV movies depict violent solutions to interpersonal conflict."

Shootings in a relatively brief time span have ravaged schools in communities as varied as Jonesboro, Arkansas; San Diego, California; Pearl, Mississippi; Paducah, Kentucky; Fayetteville, Tennessee; Pomona, California; Edinboro, Pennsylvania; Springfield, Oregon; Bethel, Alaska; and Littleton, Colorado. One young person, when asked to comment, said, "Folks don't understand teenage angst." Another responded, "The stress and self-hate encouraged in high schools push delicate teens to act out." One fifteen-year-old said, "adults today seem to think children are brazen, impetuous, unreliable, irresponsible, and uncaring. I wonder how adults think we got that way."[1]

Life is formed by two forces: the events that take place and the way in which we react to those events. Some people are laid low by relatively minor reverses, such as getting a traffic ticket or being passed over for promotion. Unavoidable losses, such as a child leaving home or the death of a parent may send them into depression. However, some are able to adjust to life's misfortunes—catastrophic illness, death of a loved one, financial collapse. The one quality that seems to separate the first group from the second is resilience. This is the ability to recover from an adverse change. The trait of bouncing back is vital to our well-being. Some persons are innately better at coping than others, but resilience isn't established at birth, for it can be enhanced or eroded later in life. When we recover from one setback it makes it easier to come back from the next. We will experience shock, the knowledge of a loss, pain, adjustment, and finally moving beyond the event. It is not easy, nor is any grief event easy, but it is vital if we are to get on with living without crippling effects.

Some persons experience the feeling that they should be immune to normal stresses, and the consequences of their own actions. Such a mind-set causes them to believe that they should get what they want, when they want, and if anyone interferes, they have a right to get them out of the way. The picture of

---
[1] *USA Weekend*, April 14–16, 2000.

young Andrew Golden with a rifle on the cover of *Time* was disturbing, as were the uncertainties about the reasons for the shooting spree in Jonesboro that he and classmate Mitchell Johnson engaged in. Psychological trauma, poor or little guidance, inadequate parenting, or bad judgment can create children ill-prepared to live in the real world; when they do not get what they think they deserve, they react with violence. And each of us is poorer because of this.

Would Gun Control Help?

Our horror knows no bounds when we read of another teenager on a murderous rampage. These recurring acts of vengeful cruelty occurring in small town America from two-parent, churchgoing, nice neighborhood families threaten our sense of safety and order. The hyper-simplistic solutions of executing them as adults or building larger prisons give us headaches and unsettled stomachs. It is difficult not to think that society is falling apart, and like "Chicken Little," we want to run and hide. Hard as it is to believe, statistics tell us that rates of violence have fallen in recent years, notably in New York and Los Angeles. But what of the school shootings? It is interesting to note the locations of some school shootings—most have been in states where the use of guns is promoted for hunting and protection. A more subtle issue is the teaching of males to avenge perceived insults and slights. The ones who have committed these murders learned early to use and value guns. An article in *The United Methodist Reporter* quotes from a source identified as Handgun Control, Inc.: "Firearms are the fourth leading cause of accidental deaths (in the United States) among children 5 to 14 years old and the third leading cause of deaths among 15 to 24-year-olds."[2] The article also cites The American Academy of Child and Adolescent Psychiatry: "Forty percent of the accidental handgun shootings of children under sixteen (in the United States) occur in the homes of friends or relatives of the child." I do not think we can file this under the heading of coincidence.

---

[2] *The United Methodist Reporter* (June 4, 1999), 4.

We need to note that the perpetrators, so far, are males. We know that there is a large chasm in the way boys and girls handle emotional issues and problems. This is especially noticeable in early adolescence. We know that, generally, adolescent females internalize anger, anxiety, or low self-esteem, frequently by developing eating disorders or becoming depressed. But adolescent males tend to externalize their problems by use of alcohol, acting out, or attacking others. Young females are more likely to talk with a friend or to play "Ain't it awful." Young males, who are usually socialized to keep all feelings inside tend to keep up a façade.

As we look at the young killers, we find no single cause for their actions. As we read the news accounts, we find some of the young men were suffering from depression, others from an obsessive-compulsive disorder. At least one seemed to be an antisocial personality; some narcissistic personality traits were evidenced, paranoia was present, and borderline tendencies were also apparent. Many of them seemed resistant to parental and school discipline, one of them had tortured animals, and they all seemed to hold a grudge and to be vulnerable to slights. Some of the boys seemed to have been dominated by a peer or a sibling; some had been the targets of bullies. All of them were evidently susceptible to holding onto hurts, perhaps magnifying those events until the idea of revenge became uppermost in their thinking. The reality of the consequences of their actions seemed absent in their planning. The grandiosity of being able to "get even" seemed paramount.

It is almost impossible for me not to see gun control as a strong deterrent to these horrifying acts. In working with suicidal persons, one of the first things therapists try to ascertain is how they plan to kill themselves and whether or not they have the means to do so. For example, if a state police detective says he would shoot himself, we know he has the method and the means to do so. If a terminally ill 90–year-old nursing home patient says she plans to shoot herself, and she has no gun or visitors, she has the desire but not the means. While we take the threat seriously, we are more concerned about her depression than about the possibility of suicide. A disturbed young man may feel slighted or mistreated, or may be unable to get out of his mind that he has been turned down by a girl. He believes he must avenge his honor. So if he has a gun in his possession or knows where he can easily steal a gun, it may be too tempting to make a statement, be invincible, and make certain no one will ever put him down again. This lonely rationalization can lead to murder and mayhem.

How Do We Respond to Violence?

Preventing violence at school starts at home. Parents need to shuck off their inhibitions that they must be careful, or their children will not like them. All parents are disliked from time to time, and I am not sure when it became a big deal. Certainly it was not one of the things my parents were concerned about. They loved their children, but the lines were drawn between parents and children. Never did the children get to be in charge; that was reserved for the parents. They knew what was in our rooms, what we read, whom we saw, if we were obsessing over not having a date or a new dress, or if my sister and I were not getting along. Of course they did not read our mail, enter without knocking, or interrupt conversations with friends, but conversation at dinner touched on issues they wished to discuss with us. Guns or home-made bombs could not have been concealed in our rooms, and we were strongly encouraged to talk about our resentments, our prejudices, and who were we, to feel we had a right to special treatment. Mealtimes hosted racial, theological, psychological, and sociological discussions, where we were encouraged to differ without rancor.

Interventions are needed if boys and girls are to learn that loneliness, anger, insecurity, despair, and anxiety will always be a part of the human condition, but that there are ways of coping other than the destruction of self or others. There are ways of being angry without either being a wuss or blowing someone away. Classes in conflict management are being held in some schools and churches. Other classes are held to counteract the pervasive teachings of popular culture that anything goes. Manners are back, and classes are taught concerning introductions, table manners, and responding to written invitations or writing thank-you notes. All schools need mental health resources, and parents need to be aware of the signs of depression in themselves and their children. Puppy love is very serious to those involved, and parents must take seriously the losses that come with growing up. This means listening, hugging, holding, being careful not to judge or put the other person down, accepting their anger, and never ignoring any threats. If you are confused or do not know what to do, seek professional help.

Learning to dialogue lets us know the whole picture, rather than a small segment of the whole. We are almost universally opposed to arguments, but we can disagree without having an argument if we follow a few principles:

- Be open to what others are saying.
- Watch all-or-nothing statements.
- Try not to affront deep moral convictions.
- Talk of needs, wants, and interests, not rights.
- Keep your own moral convictions.
- Recognize that none of us has the only truth.
- Don't embellish facts.
- Try to hear the question behind the question.
- Ask questions, but avoid questions with yes or no answers.
- Keep absolutes to a minimum.
- Strive for privacy to dialogue.
- Respect who you are talking with.

Our children need practice in learning how to rethink situations that create excessive anger. Ask them if they were deliberately left out when the others went for pizza; could there be another explanation? Did Grandma give you a lesser gift than your sister received for her birthday, or did she search for the book you told her you had to have? Did the new boy snub you, or could he not have seen you? Forgiveness should not be a foreign term to our children. Mistakes are made by all of us. None of us is perfect. Sometimes we have to ask our kids, "How long do you want to stay angry?" Learning to hear and accept criticism is vital, as well as learning how to respond to criticism. If we are defensive we can create anger. If we listen, then respond assertively, it can facilitate dialogue. Our children can be so intense, and we need to help them learn to relax. The body gives us visceral clues to our anger. Perhaps it is a headache described as a tight band around our head, a runny nose, hyperventilating, a stomachache with diarrhea, or low back pain. Often a back rub, a walk, a cool drink, or a soft voice can defuse anger and have a calming effect. It is important to understand that the constant retelling of an anger event can fuel it to a fever pitch, but a suggestion to walk away from the anger event for the time being can furnish a perspective that is absent in the heat of anger. Ask if you can arrange a time to talk about what is going on at a definite time tomorrow.

Do We Learn Our Anger?

Some of the pent-up rage that infects our society may be partly the result of our sedentary lifestyle. My grandmother put the carpets out on the clothesline each spring and beat away the winter's accumulation of dust and dirt. In the kitchen, she would grasp a bowl tight in her left arm and beat the butter and sugar with her right hand until it was creamed perfectly. My grandfather went after a horse with a bridle and saddle before he could go to the school where he taught. In later years he cranked his Model T until the motor caught and started. I have a vivid picture in my mind of my father shaking the clinkers down where they were caught in the stoker-fed furnace. My mother was always the first to hang out clothes in our neighborhood, and I can still see her bending over, grabbing a towel and giving it a hard shake before attaching it to the line with clothespins. All of these actions were natural ways of working off energy, but now our energy-saving devices do not allow this. We really have not saved energy but have stored it with no natural vents, so sometimes it explodes in acts of random violence. The radio talk shows, chat rooms on the Internet, and TV shows with angry guests, all seem to be a way to vilify one another from the safety of our homes.

If we are honest, we must face the fact that we do not handle our anger appropriately. We are appalled when our children do not know how to deal with their anger, but the apple does not fall far from the tree. Where do our children learn about anger? How can they learn that anger is a good gift if used properly? When they are in car with you, do they see you cut off another car because it cut in front of you? When you do not get your own way, do your children see you throw inanimate objects and hear you hurl words at whoever is present? Do you cry or pout when you do not get your way? Have you ever refused to return to a church meeting because your ideas were not accepted? Is there any person in your family whom you do not talk with, and if he or she will be at a family gathering, you do not attend? Do you have a sense of entitlement that allows you to be angry with others, but they cannot be angry with you? Do you have a gun in your home, but deplore the escalating violence in our society? Are we as guiltless about the escalating violence as we pretend to be?

Problems in communication frequently lead to anger. The person who proudly proclaims never to be angry is simply not communicating the anger—at least not in words. Body language shows the denied anger—a set jaw, flashing eyes, rigid posture. One of my clients calls such body langauge "silent yelling," which she says is what her father engages in when he is unhappy. She says he has this down to a fine science, where the whole household becomes an armed camp, waiting while dad holds them all hostage. The lack of communication—an implied virtue because he does not speak words of anger—the tense atmosphere, and the absence of resolution combine in what she aptly calls silent yelling.

All children need to have an opportunity to develop their personal styles of dealing with anger. Families are a crucible where emotions peak and wane and are an ideal environment to learn ways of anger that are both Christian and workable. The screamer learns to takef time to cool off before blowing off steam all over the place. The withdrawn, quiet child learns to appropriately express anger vocally. Whatever the personal style, children learn how to release anger in safe and effective ways. We play a key role in teaching children how to deal with other people's tempers as well as their own. Always acknowledge your child's anger. You do not have to fix it, but accept the feelings, even if you do not think the anger is justified. Teach children how to use words to express how they feel, and suggest that they hit a pillow or roll up a newspaper and hit a table, anything that relieves the intensity but does not hurt anyone. Be free with your praise when disagreements are settled without hitting.

We need to look at how we expect our children to handle anger constructively and nonviolently if we hit them ourselves. Studies tell us that children who are spanked or whipped are more likely to exhibit antisocial behavior later. This is not the only factor, but it is a contributor. Your pediatrician can suggest alternatives to physical punishment. Time-outs, sending a child to his or her room, or withdrawing a favorite toy are effective and do not demean a child. With older children, I like to ask them what they feel is an appropriate discipline for their behavior. I like to avoid use of pejorative words such as *bad,* or *mean,* and also to avoid calling a child a problem child or comparing them unfavorably with another child or adult. Rules need to be few and clear, with no hitting allowed. Let children work out problems themselves if possible, and intervene only when things get out of hand. If you watch violent movies, TV, or videos, talk with your children about how the characters could have settled their disputes without hurting others. If your child is confronted by a bully, make sure your child knows a bully is basically a coward who likes to see others cry. It is most effective if they can just walk away. There is safety in numbers, and a child who is with friends is less likely to be a target of bullying. Always report bullying behavior to the teacher or other persons in authority. Try to be calm when your child tells you about such an incident, as children take their clues about how to behave from you.

Some Teaching Tools

Anger management programs are effective. Such programs as "Chill Out" in Los Angeles and "Second Step" in Seattle teach children self-control, empathy, and respect for others. For information on organizing a conflict-resolution program write to the National Institute for Dispute Resolution, 1726 M Street NW, Suite 500, Washington, DC 20036–4502.

The American Academy of Pediatrics and the American Psychological Association offer a pamphlet called "Raising Children to Resist Violence." To receive this, send a business-size stamped, self-addressed envelope to the American Academy of Pediatrics, Department C–Violence, 141 Northwest Point Boulevard, P.O. Box 927, Elk Grove, IL 60009–0927. The Hazelden Institute has videos to use with groups, including

"How to Teach Kids to Handle Anger Without Violence." For more information, call 1–800–231–5165.

Distinguishing reality from fantasy and facts, and from commercial fluff, is critical. Unfortunately, young television viewers can't always tell the difference. The National Cable Television Association, in partnership with the Girl Scouts of America, offers "TV Smarts for Kids." This is a free, three-part video that teaches basic media literacy skills. Part I, is for children 5 to 7 years old, and asks, "What Is TV All About?" The video encourages children to see television as being made of three parts: make believe, real people and events, and commercials. Part II, for children 8 to 11, is called, "How Does TV Make Things Look Different?" Part III, for youths 12 to 17, asks, "Why Do People Watch TV?" To obtain a video, contact your local cable company or the Girl Scout Council, or write the National Cable Television Association, Public Affairs Department, 1724 Massachusetts Ave. NW, Washington, DC 20036.

When children are angry, ask them to name the feeling they are experiencing. They may need you to suggest several feelings, such as mad, sad, glad, surprised, angry, upset, frustrated, or bothered. Then ask them to identify the object or person associated with their anger. Most often this is a person who has caused them to be denied some pleasure. This person may be you. Be accepting if the child is angry with you. With older children, ask them to write a letter to the person and express their anger, even if that person lives in their own home. Since these letters are not mailed, they can be completely honest. If they want to share their letter or mail it, ask them to wait two or three days and then talk about it with you first. With young children, ask them to draw their feelings, and then ask them to tell you about their picture. The letters or the drawings both give permission to be angry in a way that honors the feelings, but in no way condones violence. It helps children to know that being mad is not a weakness or a crime, and learning to manage and express anger can be an opportunity to grow. Be alert for behavioral warning signs such as social withdrawal, acting like a victim, feeling persecuted, low grades, talk of violence, intense anger, discipline problems, and/or extreme prejudice.

As children grow and develop, encourage them to express their feelings by keeping a diary or starting a journal. This is the beginning of a therapeutic dialogue with the inner self. The gift of a diary or a journal to a school-age child encourages the child to accept his or her foibles and imperfections, as well as celebrate joys and successes. To write about shame, anger, or being put down is to place it in the conscious mind rather than have it smolder in the unconscious. Encourage the expression of emotions by your children, remembering agreement is not as important as honoring the expression of their feelings. Remind them that feelings are not good or bad, right or wrong; feelings just are.

Putting It All Together

Children today are angry. This is not all bad, if we can teach them to use their anger constructively. Of course, for this to happen we must learn to identify our own anger and find healthy and appropriate ways of dealing with it. Adults may find it helpful to put a punching bag in the basement or garage to try to dredge up old angers. Keeping a journal to note emotions, your reactions, and how you coped can be an eye-opener. If anger remains a problem, despite your efforts to work it out, then it is time to seek help from your pastor, a counselor, or a mental health professional. Joining a group for assertiveness training or conflict-resolution gives you tools to deal with anger at home, church, school, sports, or your workplace.

Humor can be an aid in dealing with anger—your own or that of others. I worked with a client who seemed to be devoid of humor. He could not accept a joke and satire seemed to go over his head. This lack of humor and an inability to laugh at himself were causing problems in his marriage and at his place of employment. I assigned him some books to read, cartoons to watch, and videos and movies to see, and asked him to report his observations to me. It was slow going, but eventually he found a sense of humor buried under his work ethic and his old memories. At breakfast one morning he inadvertently poured tomato juice on his cereal. His wife awaited the blow-up, but to her surprise, and his also, he burst out laughing, saying, "I bet you never tried tomato juice on your shredded wheat." They both laughed until they cried, and then they used it as a catch phrase to describe a bad day or a foolish choice. Such events can become shorthand in families to help us accept our humanity, and that it is all right not to be perfect.

As parents, we need to be aware as soon as possible when the behavior of our children is unusual. Sullen, morose, depressed, and perpetually angry children are a wake-up call to parents that all is not well.

Look for the symptoms of depression: change in eating habits, crying, sleeping too much or too little, feeling hopeless, giving away possessions, being secretive, having difficulty making decisions, not wanting to go out, or spending most of their time alone. When a usually extroverted child becomes withdrawn, it is a warning. The same is true of a usually introverted child now acting out of character. Red-flag such changes in your own mind, and consult your spouse, your child's teacher, church school teacher, pediatrician, or scout leader.

We cannot eliminate all the violence in our world, but we can provide an atmosphere without violence in our homes and schools. Some leading child development experts believe that it is vital that children be protected from video games that glorify violence. Aggressive images have been known to "hop up" children's nervous systems and give them an adrenaline rush that they crave to repeat. Shooting people on a computer screen is even more harmful than watching people get gunned down on TV. The experts agree that passive watching is engaging, but when it is active it gets the motor system involved, which raises the risk that a child will adapt that behavior. Parents should seek games that promote team building, sharing, and problem solving. Rethinking situations in our homes that could be construed as violent, will be necessary if we are to create homes that are an antithesis to our violent, gun owning, angry, belligerent society. We need to create a society where we are free to be angry, in appropriate ways, and we need to get angry enough to press for societal change. We must guard our anger from petty use and destructive expressions. Embrace your anger as a God-given emotion. Anger is a deep emotion that signals all is not well. Use it well as one of God's good gifts.

8

Practical Advice for Claiming the Gift of Anger

Several years ago, I flew into Dallas-Fort Worth late in the evening. I picked up my rental car and left the airport complex. When I was on the freeway I began to experience problems steering the car. It was late, and I elected to go on to my hotel, since I was about halfway between the airport and my hotel. When I arrived I called about the car, and the agency sent me a replacement the next morning, with apologies. The car I was given in error had a tire that was "out of round," causing it to be unbalanced and thus hard to steer. Since it did not appear to the eye to have a problem, it had been mistakenly rented out.

I think of this sometimes when I see lives that are so completely out of balance. Electrolytes out of balance cause great difficulties physically, leading to weakness and nausea. We had a friend who lost a big toe to surgery, and virtually had to learn to walk again because his balance was off. It's such a small thing to carry so many consequences, but the matter of *balance* is not a small thing. Let's look at what is out of balance in our life.

Balance

What is out of balance in my life? Is it my health? my safety? my comfort? my behavior? my success or lack of success? my addiction? my self-esteem? my depression?

What about my career, what is out of balance there? Is it my performance? my future? my workaholic style? the people I work with? the fear I am getting nowhere?

What's out of balance in my family (immediate family and extended family)? Is it an ascribed role? being taken for granted? by finances? being in charge when anything goes wrong? having to be the family troubleshooter or chaplain?

Am I out of balance in my neighborhood and community? In what way? Environmental issues? Political matters? Social concerns? Education? Taxes?

How am I out of balance in global issues? Natural resources? Peace with justice? The haves and the have-nots? Human rights? War?

What is out of balance in ultimate life issues? Your faith? Your call to service? Your commitment? Your trust? Alienation? Feeling you are far from God?

What Controls My Life?

This is a quick survey to enable you to take a look at what controls your life. How often do you experience the following things? Answer each with a number from 0 to 6, with 0 for rarely, 3 for sometimes, and 6 for often.

___ I have difficulty knowing my feelings.

___ I have difficulty expressing my feelings.

___ My life is one crisis after another.

___ I have too much responsibility.

___ People irritate me.

___ I spend a lot of time worrying.

___ Everyone makes too many demands on me.

___ I do not have enough time for myself.

___ I am concerned about the future.

___ Focusing is hard for me.

___ Communication is a problem for me.

___ I get too little support from others.

___ I never get done what I need to do.

___ I don't have enough say about decisions that affect me.
___ Others keep me from doing what I want to do.
___ I feel fatigued much of the time.
___ I drink too much coffee.
___ I frequently overeat, especially fats and sweets.
___ I drink to wind down.
___ I smoke.
___ I get too little physical exercise.
___ I feel the need to make life changes, but I don't know how.
___ SCORE

    40–65: Some changes needed
    65–95: Think seriously about life changes
    95 or more: Make changes *now*!

Who controls your life? Who makes your decisions? It is easy to get into the habit of letting others make decisions for you, or it can be *easier* to let others make decisions for you, so that you are never responsible for what happens. Ultimately each of us is responsible for our own choices, and then responsible for what happens, even if we have made a poor choice. This is free will. If you have been turning this responsibility over to others, now is the time to take back and retain what is yours. Your decision, your choice, your responsibility, your life—you are the only person with the control.

Breathing

Anger, rage, hatred can almost stop our breathing, or at least cause us to take shallow, quick, uneven breaths. It is too easy to hyperventilate, become dizzy, or lightheaded. Breathing properly can improve one's well-being, both physically and emotionally. Try this:

1. Breathe in (inhale) to the count of four.
2. Hold your breath to the count of four.
3. Breathe out (exhale) to the count of eight. (Do not exhale rapidly. Exhale very slowly and rhythmically.)

Associate breathing with another task
- Each time you look at your watch, take an extra deep breath.
- When you brush your teeth, remember to breathe deeply.
- As you turn on your car's ignition, take time to breathe deeply.
- As you warm up before exercising, breathe deeply.
- As you enter into a quiet time with God, breathe deeply.
- As you look into the mirror, breathe deeply.
- (Use the 4–4–8 count as you breathe.)

Breathing to Increase Concentration

Take five deep breaths using the 4–4–8 count. Always breathe slowly and steadily. Concentrate on your breathing. If you can't concentrate, begin your five deep breaths again.

Conflict Management

Many myths have grown up around anger, and like most myths they are often accepted as gospel. One of those myths is that anger is triggered automatically, which causes persons to become victims of their own anger. The second myth is that anger must be expressed, that we must let it all out no matter who it hurts. If you are living either of these myths, it is my prayer that you will examine them and see how poorly they are serving you, and how they are causing problems in your interactions with others. Many people tell me they cannot control their anger, but of course we can—not instantly or perfectly, but we can choose not to carry around anger like a prize. If we continue to act on the belief that anger is uncontrollable, then we create a way to avoid being responsible for our own actions. It is a cop-out of the first order, even if you think it may have been working for you. How much easier to blame others, than to take a long hard look at self.

Choosing how we will deal with our anger goes beyond pushing it deep inside to keep it from showing, blasting everyone within range of our voice, or taking refuge in our tears. It is vital that we look inward to see the payoff of out-of-control anger. Perhaps we find that people pay attention when we are uncontrollably angry; for at least a few moments, we are the priority to which they must give their full attention. In this way you find anger rewarding, since much anger originates when we feel we are not being taken seriously. Our self-image wants to be important, and we may have old memories of feelings when insulted. Whether we really were insulted is not as important as how we perceived what was happening. Since perceptions are frequently motivated by our old tapes, irrational anger may result. If we are motivated to look inward, we can discover what has happened to us, what we have been taught, and the old tapes we are holding sacred. If this seems too difficult, find a counselor who can guide you in this process. Hatred may last, resentment can endure, dissatisfaction and frustration can be a lifetime companion and unless you really want to learn to be all that God created you to be, by learning the truth.

If we are to deal in a healthy way with what creates conflict, we must recognize that we have choices with our anger. If we can acknowledge we have some control over our anger, if we make a decision not to sullenly protect our anger, if we truly want to learn to work with our response to anger; then we can view anger as natural and inevitable, without giving it a bad label. If we are honest, we learn that while others might stimulate our anger, we are the ones to make an appropriate response to our feelings. We can use our anger in a positive way, or we can go on seeing ourselves as a victim of helplessness and mistreatment. Being a victim will not resolve conflict, nor will wishful thinking. Most colleges and universities, as well as many counseling and mental health centers, regularly conduct classes in conflict management. They are extremely helpful, if you are motivated to go, rather than going to please another person. Acting out our anger in an aggressive way frequently inflames our anger, rather than reducing it.

Talking with a good friend, pastor, or a trained counselor can be helpful, but avoid those who inflame your anger and increase your aggressive bent. This does not reduce your anger but turns it into rage and your decisions are then less than rational. Talking does not give you solutions, but should open up your options so you can work through your feelings, and make a choice of how you wish to deal with your anger. In marital conflicts it is helpful to explain your position and then carefully listen while your partner explains his or hers. The idea is not to be right or to win, but to gain understanding. I once had a client who changed jobs frequently, and his wife went into orbit each time this happened. Their pattern in marital fighting was to try to out-shout each other. Clearly this brought much heat to their discussion, but no resolution. I was about ready to get a whip and a chair to restore order when they argued in my office, but I decided to reinforce their listening by using a timer where each spoke for 30 seconds and the other had 30 seconds to say what they heard being said. It was amazing what they heard for the first time. He said he did not know she was petrified when he changed jobs, for security to her meant staying with a position. She did not know he felt trapped if he stayed with a company too long. Knowledge is power, and both learned to look underneath feelings to understand the dynamics involved.

I had a professor who used to quote Aristotle, "Anger is hot and seeks to injure; hatred is cold and seeks to destroy." If anger is used as a weapon, there is injury, retaliation, and withdrawal, none of which are helpful in working through our emotions. Anger can become a problem when we argue and the anger triggered becomes the problem rather than the issue. Anger by itself is never successful in negotiating. Anger, like pain, means there is something in your life that needs attention. This symptom must be taken seriously. I need to add that no matter how well you know yourself and your anger response, constant bickering, nagging, or complaining may overload your circuits. This is the time to look at such chronic behavior with your situation at home, work, church, or community environment. If you map out a plan to address the bickering, then work until a solution is found, you have made progress. If there is a stalemate and the conflict cannot be resolved, you must seek new avenues of redress.

Being Free from Anger

We all long for the "peace that passes all understanding," but is it to be ours in this lifetime? What happens when your spouse, coworker, a customer, a neighbor, or even a stranger comes at you with anger? Do you respond with more anger? It seems more expedient to switch to a controlled response, rather than enter into a verbal brawl. It may be difficult not to respond either defensively or offensively, but work to give them feedback and try to verbalize their anger. ("I hear your anger, and you feel we did not take your complaint seriously. Can you tell us again of your concern?") Most persons who verbally abuse you with their anger want you to know how angry they are, and in essence to hand over their problem to you, indicating this is all your fault. If you can hold off on your response, listen carefully, and give a nonjudgmental response, hopefully you can hold the problem where it is, without it accelerating. The high level of anger is defused as the angry person is assured you have heard her or him. You have heard the other person's feelings, neither accepted nor rejected them, made no judgments, and you have not aggravated the fight.

Most people welcome an opportunity to move back from their anger once they feel they have been granted a hearing. The other person is expecting you to counter with anger or to make a strategic retreat; if you do neither, you are in control. The force of the attack lessens as you listen and give feedback, without accepting the problem as your own. Another time when I was traveling, I arrived late one night to find my reserved room at the hotel was not available. The clerk was angry and began with a volley of words about the mix-up. I let him run out of words and calmly repeated back what he had said. We went through this twice before he stopped, and agreed to let me have a suite for the same price as my reserved room. He obviously felt he was the fall guy for someone else's mistake and was very defensive. It was not my anger, so I reflected it back by assuring him I had heard him, but in no way did I accept his anger as mine. It was late and I was travel-weary. I had a presentation to do very early the next morning. It would have been easy to have a shouting match with the clerk, which would have energized the confrontation, leaving me with my adrenaline surging. I made the choice that enabled me to meet my needs without tramping on the clerk's needs.

We always have options and choices when we are angry. We may not like the options, but we have them. We can allow others to walk all over us, we can fight dirty, or we can learn how to enter the skirmish listening to what is really being said—and take the option where there are no winners or losers. When we blast someone, cut her down to size, humiliate him, we have almost certainly damaged the relationship and the issue remains unsolved. It is sad for me to attend an anniversary party and hear the couple say, "We never disagree or get angry." First off, I do not believe them, and then I want to say, "Why not?" Disagreeing reveals needs, wounds, and problem areas that are in every committed relationship. The people we love the most often produce the most anger, because we care enough to disagree with them, and aspire for them to know what is important to us. Besides, without arguments and disagreements, we miss the joy of making up, achieving compromises, better understanding, and increased intimacy.

We cannot ever be free from anger, nor should we aspire to that goal. This would be saying that nothing is ever worth fighting for. This does not mean we must be in a state of constant contention. It does mean we must look at old angers that trip a switch and cause us to react over an issue that is not worth overextending our energy supply. It means we must look at our choices and decide how we will respond when we are attacked, mistreated, or abused. It also means we must give up the fairy tale that some white knight or fairy godmother is going to come and make everything all right for us. We have the gift and glory of free will; we choose, and then we live with the consequences of that choice. I'm guessing that many women buy the idea of submitting to their husbands' decision-making, because then they do not have to be responsible for any choices made. The buck never stops with them, as they have abandoned and negated their responsibility. Mutual submission creates mutual decisions and mutual living with choices made to benefit both.

Wrapping It All Up

Being angry is a choice. How we act out our anger is our decision. No one can *make* me angry. I make the choice and then I am responsible for the choice I made. No one is free from anger, even those people who say they never get angry. Anger is a good, God-given emotion, and we need to use this gift wisely. We need openness and honesty in looking inward to see the sources of our anger. When we are suddenly angry, out of proportion to what has happened, we must examine ourselves to find the genesis of such anger. For example, why such a reaction to a minor event? Could guilt be a factor? Could my anxiety about a number of events be coloring my reaction? Is it possible my anger about my work situation is spilling over into my personal life? If your answers to these questions are not satisfactory, then seek some outside help.

Living life to the fullest demands we search and find *balance* in all parts of our daily life. Balance requires a long, hard look at the way we are living our lives. What causes confusion is when we give lip service to one area of life as being most important, but a comparison of time spent in that area reveals something else entirely. If we claim our children are our first priority, but never can find time to be with them in their varied interests, how believable do our words sound? In the language of Alcoholics Anonymous, we must not only be able to "talk the talk, but walk the walk." If our anger is a problem in our life, causing reprimands at work, dissension in our homes, and isolation from friends, we need professional help. Seeking out the help you need is not a weakness, but a great strength.

It is important to find out what controls my life. Is it money, power, prestige, fame, attention, or wanting everyone to love me? If we rush through life without ever slowing down to see if we are headed in the right direction, then that is the controlling element in our life. Or if we have given the power of our lives over to someone else—we may never get blamed, but then we miss the challenge of setting a goal and reaching that goal. Perhaps you need to make life changes, but the rut you are in is very comfortable—so you stay put, carrying a load of regrets without ever knowing if you could have achieved your dream.

Other emotions do influence our anger. Guilt, which has been termed the emotional cancer of relationships, is so subtle, yet so pervasive. When we take responsibility for other people's feelings, thoughts, or behavior, a toxic relationship develops and the rules of relationship are changed. We are responsible only for our feelings and actions. The actions and feelings of others are their own. If we are to do more than survive, we must strive to be the same person inside and out, content to be ourselves without wasting time maintaining a facade or trying to conceal our "shadow" side. Knowing that our identity is not dependent on external factors, we must be willing to accept responsibility and not think of adverse circumstances as making us a victim. When we make a mistake, we acknowledge it and move on. We must be open to change, for change is one of the constants in life, often presenting new opportunities. Flexibility to adapt leaves us open to respond. We need faith in ourselves in order to rise to the daily challenges. A sense of purpose beyond ourselves produces the unflagging conviction that life is worth living.

Knowing when we are angry is vital if we are to be fully aware of our emotions and the impact they have on our lives. We will never be free from anger because we are human, and we need our anger to fight prejudice, to stand up for what we believe, and to let us know when something in the system is not working. We have various options as to how we get to the other side of our anger. Our anger is one of God's good gifts, and we must be accountable for our response to it.